FIRSTS, LASTS
& ONLYS®

"Donnelley is the master of
reference books"

– Mitchell Symons

"Paul Donnelley is one of the
world's leading oddity hunters"

– Jeremy Beadle

Firsts, lasts & onlys®

THE MOST AMAZING

RUGBY

FACTS FROM PAST TO PRESENT

PAUL DONNELLEY

First published by Pitch Publishing, 2015

Pitch Publishing
A2 Yeoman Gate
Yeoman Way
Durrington
BN13 3QZ
www.pitchpublishing.co.uk

A CIP catalogue record is available for this book from the British Library

ISBN 978-1-78531- 038-6

Typesetting and origination by Pitch Publishing
Printed by Bell & Bain, Glasgow

THE FIRSTS

THE LASTS

THE ONLYS

Dedication

Dedicated to the "Serious Girl"
who makes me laugh more than
any other.

Acknowledgements

I would like to thank the following for their help, inspiration and kindness, whether they realised it or not: Sue Beadle; Gavin Fuller of the Telegraph Media Group; Robert Gate; John Godber; Ian Harrison; Phil Harrison; Andrew Hardcastle; Gary Hetherington; Ian Jackson; Thomas Keenes; Stuart Leadley; Mitchell Symons; John Williams, Liverpool St Helens Press Officer; Linda Yaffe.

Paul Donnelley, 2015
www.pauldonnelley.com

NOTE: Throughout I have referred to firsts, lasts and onlys of "rugby" or "rugby football" where they apply to either code, and of rugby union or rugby league where they apply to rugby union or rugby league only. Note also that in rugby league Test matches British teams were billed as England until 1948 when they were billed as Great Britain.

FIRST

PERSON TO TAKE THE BALL IN HIS ARMS AND RUN WITH IT

WILLIAM WEBB ELLIS AT SCHOOL CLOSE, RUGBY SCHOOL, WARWICKSHIRE CV22 5EH ENGLAND. (APOCRYPHAL) 1823.

William Webb Ellis's act of rule-breaking, which supposedly gave birth to the game of rugby football as we know it, has been commemorated with a plaque at Rugby School, a £40,000 bronze statue in Rugby town, and the naming of the Rugby Union World Cup after him. Yet there is no evidence that Ellis ever committed the act for which he is so famous. The source of the story is two letters from Matthew Bloxham, an Old Rugbeian and antiques dealer, to the Rugby School magazine, *The Meteor*. In the first, dated 10 October 1876, he wrote that he had discovered that the change from a kicking game to a handling one had "... originated with a town boy or foundationer of the name of Ellis, Webb Ellis". Bloxham said that Webb Ellis had handled the ball in 1824. Four years later, on 22 December 1880, he wrote again and added more detail including changing the year of the event to 1823, one year earlier. Bloxham states that the Manchester-born Ellis joined the school in 1816 at the age of nine, and that:

> "A boy of the name Ellis – William Webb Ellis – a town boy and a foundationer, ... whilst playing Bigside at football in that half-year [1823], caught the ball in his arms. This being so, according to the then rules, he ought to have retired back

as far as he pleased, without parting with the ball, for the combatants on the opposite side could only advance to the spot where he had caught the ball, and were unable to rush forward till he had either punted it or had placed it for some one else to kick, for it was by means of these placed kicks that most of the goals were in those days kicked, but the moment the ball touched the ground the opposite side might rush on. Ellis, for the first time, disregarded this rule, and on catching the ball, instead of retiring backwards, rushed forwards with the ball in his hands towards the opposite goal, with what result as to the game I know not, neither do I know how this infringement of a well-known rule was followed up, or when it became, as it is now, a standing rule."

Even if this is true, the idea did not immediately catch on, and "running in" tries did not become accepted practice until the 1830s, by which time Ellis had graduated from Oxford University and taken Holy Orders. He died, unmarried, in the south of France on 24 February 1872. He left £9,000 with some of it going to a society for abandoned women and children. William Webb Ellis was then lost to history until October 1959 when Ross McWhirter (1925-1975), the author and the co-founder of *The Guinness Book Of Records*, and Roger Driès, the former player, discovered his grave in the cemetery of the Vieux Chateau in Menton, where the French Rugby Union provided a new grave. A plaque commemorating Ellis's mythical act was erected at Rugby School in around 1900. It reads:

THIS STONE
COMMEMORATES THE EXPLOIT OF
WILLIAM WEBB ELLIS
WHO WITH A FINE DISREGARD FOR THE RULES OF
FOOTBALL
AS PLAYED IN HIS TIME
FIRST TOOK THE BALL IN HIS HANDS AND RAN WITH IT
THUS ORIGINATING THE DISTINCTIVE FEATURE OF
THE RUGBY GAME
A.D. 1823

FIRST
LAWS OF THE GAMES

WILLIAM DELAFIELD ARNOLD, W.W. SHIRLEY AND FREDERICK HUTCHINS, SIXTH FORM PUPILS OF RUGBY SCHOOL, WARWICKSHIRE CV22 5EH ENGLAND. THURSDAY 28 AUGUST 1845.

The Rugby Football Union may not have been founded until after the Football Association but the rules of rugby were codified three years earlier than those of the round ball game. The first set of rules was drawn up on 25 August 1845, approved three days later by a committee of Sixth Form pupils, and printed in Rugby by printer J.S. Crossley, its title page proudly stating:

FOOTBALL RULES

THE FOLLOWING

Rules

WERE SANCTIONED BY A LEVÉE OF THE SIXTH,

On the 28th of August, 1845,

As the

LAWS OF FOOTBALL

PLAYED

At Rugby School

The thirty-seven rules included many terms still in use, such as offside, knock-on, punt, touch and try at goal. However, some rules are no longer relevant, including rule 20 – "All matches are drawn after five days, but after three if no goal has been kicked" – and rule 18: "A player having touched the ball straight for a tree, and touched the tree with it, may drop from either side if he can."

FIRST
REGULAR MANUFACTURERS
OF RUGBY BALLS

William Gilbert and Richard Lindon at Lawrence Sheriff Street,
Rugby, Warwickshire, England. 1840s.

The shape and size of the ball were not written into the rules until
1892, by which time the distinctive oval shape had long been the norm.
The balls used by Rugby School, being encased in leather, were made,
naturally enough, by two local boot- and shoemakers: Lindon (1816-
87), who claimed to have invented the distinctive shaped rugby ball but
never patented it, and Gilbert (1799-1877), who exhibited a ball at the
Great Exhibition of 1851 and whose firm remains a major manufacturer
to this day. The oval shape of the ball is said to have originated from the
elongated shape of the pigs' bladders used to inflate the balls. These were
superseded in the 1860s by India rubber bladders, which enabled the
oval shape to be made more exaggerated in order to facilitate handling
and passing. Rubber bladders also put an end to tragedies such as that of
Lindon's wife, who died of a lung disease thought to have been brought
on by the years she spent blowing into pigs' bladders to inflate the rugby
balls made by her husband.

FIRST
MENTION OF RUGBY
IN WALES

St David's College, College Street, Lampeter SA48 7ED Wales. 1850.

In 1850, Old Etonian Reverend Rowland Williams (1817-70) became
vice-principal of St David's College, Lampeter where he also taught
Hebrew and introduced the game to the principality. The Reverend Mr
Williams had previously been a tutor at King's College, Cambridge, when
Old Rugbeian Arthur Pell brought the sport to King's and Cambridge.
The red strip that is sported by Wales was originally worn by the college
side and they are the only club permitted to wear it.

FIRST

MENTION OF RUGBY
IN SCOTLAND

EDINBURGH, SCOTLAND. 1854.

In 1854, the brothers Francis and Alexander Crombie moved to Edinburgh from their home in Durham. Francis attended Edinburgh Academy and Alexander set up the Edinburgh Academical Football Club in 1857 and from 1858 until 1864 he was captain. Around the same time and coincidentally rugby began to be played at the Royal High School when an English boy named Hamilton enrolled bringing with him a set of the first Rules of Rugby Football. **The first match between schools** occurred on 13 February 1858 and was between Merchiston and Royal High School.

FIRST

MENTION OF RUGBY
IN A NOVEL

Thomas Hughes, Tom Brown's School Days, *published by Macmillan at London, England. Friday 24 April 1857.*

Originally published pseudonymously by "An Old Boy of Rugby", *Tom Brown's School Days* contains a detailed description of a football match at Rugby School with well over a hundred players. After the kick-off, "the two sides close, and you can see nothing for minutes but a swaying crowd of boys, at one point violently agitated. That is where the ball is, and there are the keen players to be met, and the glory and hard knocks to be got… This is what we call 'a scrummage', gentlemen, and the first scrummage in a School-house match was no joke". Then Hughes describes some of the finer points of a game with many recognisable aspects: "chargers" (forwards), "dodgers" (half-backs), and "quarters" (three-quarters and full-backs); shouts of "off your side" and "in touch"; a lineout, and a touchdown under the posts. But there are no points scored for the touch-down – the ball is kicked out from under the posts to a team-mate who "strikes his heel into the ground to mark the spot where the ball was caught, beyond which the [opposition] may not advance: but there they stand, ready to rush the moment the ball touches the ground". The catcher then retreats from the mark and places the ball for the kicker to attempt a goal before the opposition can charge him down. The ball sails over the crossbar and the cheers ring out: "A goal in the first hour – such a thing hasn't been done in the School-house match these five years".

Note: The first mention of rugby in any form of fiction came in a twenty-four-page booklet published in 1851, entitled *Football: The First Day Of The Sixth Match* (i.e., Sixth Form match), and written by William Delafield Arnold (1828-59), the fourth son of the Rugby School headmaster Thomas Arnold. William Arnold was part of the "levée of Bigside" which drew up the first rules in 1845 (see page 17).

DID YOU KNOW?

Thomas Hughes was a social reformer as well as a novelist, and on 5 October 1880 he founded the cooperative, class-free, agricultural community of Rugby, Tennessee, for Englishmen wanting to start a new life in America.

FIRST
OPEN RUGBY CLUB
LIVERPOOL FC, AIGBURTH ROAD, LIVERPOOL, MERSEYSIDE L19 3QF ENGLAND. FOUNDED SATURDAY 19 DECEMBER 1857.

Known simply as Liverpool Football Club, because it was founded before the Football Association and the Rugby Football Union, Liverpool was the first "open" club in the sense that it was not restricted to members of a school, university or other organisation. It came into existence when

Old Rugbeian Frank Albert Mather invited his friend Richard Sykes, then captain of football at Rugby School, to bring a Lindon football (see 1840s) to Liverpool Cricket Club at Edge Hill for a game of rugby football. Some fifty players turned up and Mather organised the match as Rugby (i.e. Rugbeians and Old Rugbeians) v The World. The score is not recorded although five goals were said to have been scored but by whom is not known. The game proved popular enough to warrant forming a club immediately after the game. In 1860 Sykes helped to found the Manchester Club. He later emigrated to the USA, where he founded five towns in North Dakota. He died at Santa Barbara, California, on 31 May 1923, the centenary of the mythical invention of rugby. In 1986, Liverpool FC merged with St Helens to become Liverpool St Helens Football Club.

DID YOU KNOW?

The Rugby Football Union accepts that the first rugby club was Guy's Hospital, founded in London in 1843.

FIRST

SPORT TO DERIVE DIRECTLY FROM RUGBY

Australian Rules Football. Saturday 31 July 1858.

Australian Thomas Wentworth Wills (1835-80) was educated at Rugby School from February 1850, where he was noted more for his cricketing prowess than his footballing skills. When he returned to Australia, arriving in Melbourne on 23 December 1856, Wills gained a reputation as one of the best cricketers in Victoria, and on 10 July 1858 a letter from the eminent cricketer was published in *Bell's Life in Victoria & Sporting Chronicle*:

> "Now that cricket has been put aside for some few months to come, and cricketers have assumed somewhat of the chrysalis

nature (for a time only 'tis true), but at length will again burst forth in all their varied hues, rather than allow this state of torpor to creep over them, and stifle their new supple limbs, why can they not, I say, form a foot-ball club, and form a committee of three or four to draw up a code of laws?"

Wills signed off by saying he trusted "that someone will take up the matter" but in the end he did so himself, organising an experimental match at the Richmond Paddock (later known as Yarra Park) on 31 July – the first recorded game of Australian football. The oldest surviving set of laws was drawn up on 17 May 1859 at the Parade Hotel, East Melbourne, by a committee including Wills, who reputedly wanted to adopt Rugby School rules wholesale. In the end the rules were adapted for the drier Australian climate, one of the most significant differences being the lack of an offside rule. Wills played more than two hundred and ten games, mainly for Geelong, until his retirement in 1876. Wills's gravestone describes him as "Founder of Australian Football and Champion Cricketer of his time".

DID YOU KNOW?

Tom Wills and his father, Horatio, both met violent deaths. Horatio Wills was the sixth son of Edward Spencer Wills who had been transported for life for highway robbery. In 1861, at the height of his fame, Wills and his father trekked to Queensland where they intended to establish a family property at Cullin-la-Ringo. On 17 October, a fortnight after their arrival, Horatio Wills and eighteen others including women and children were murdered by Aborigines using nulla nullas in the largest massacre of European settlers in Australian history. Tom Wills was born just too early for international cricket, playing his last first class match in 1876, a year before the first Test. He enjoyed a drink but drank too deeply and too often. On 2 May 1880 at his Heidelberg, Melbourne home, he stabbed himself to death with a pair of scissors, plunging them into his heart three times. An inquest returned a verdict of suicide while of unsound mind caused by excessive drinking.

ONLY

FOOTBALL CLUB TO BE A FOUNDER MEMBER
OF BOTH THE FOOTBALL ASSOCIATION
AND THE RUGBY
FOOTBALL UNION

BLACKHEATH FC, LONDON, ENGLAND. MONDAY 26 OCTOBER 1863.

In 1863, football and rugby parted ways after the captain of Barnes FC wrote to the sporting weekly *Bell's Life* suggesting: "…it is advisable that a football association should be formed for the purpose of settling a code of rules for the regulation of the game of football". The first meeting of the Football Association took place on 26 October when the following eleven clubs met in the Freemason's Tavern, Long Acre, London: Blackheath School; Barnes; Blackheath; Crystal Palace; Crusaders; Forest of Leytonstone (later to become Wanderers and the first winners of the FA Cup); Kensington School; N.N. Club (N.N. stood for No Names and they came from Kilburn); Perceval House of Blackheath; Surbiton and War Office. The proposed rules of "football" – which still included handling but banned hacking and tripping – were discussed at a meeting on 14 November and F.W. Campbell of Blackheath declared them "worthy of consideration". However, on 1 December, Campbell stated that hacking was an essential element of football, and on 8 December he withdrew Blackheath from the Football Association. Without the influence of Blackheath and other such clubs, yet more aspects of the Rugby School game were dropped and the remaining FA members developed the new, non-handling game of association football.

DID YOU KNOW?

The first game of football played under FA rules took place on 19 December 1863 between Barnes FC and Richmond FC at Mortlake. Richmond almost immediately withdrew from the FA, and on 2 January 1864 drew with Blackheath in what would become rugby's first – and still rugby union's oldest – regular fixture.

FIRST
NATIONAL ORGANISATION FOR RUGBY

RUGBY FOOTBALL UNION AT PALL MALL RESTAURANT,
1 COCKSPUR STREET, WESTMINSTER, LONDON SW1
ENGLAND. THURSDAY 26 JANUARY 1871.

The Rugby Football Union (RFU) was initiated by Richmond Football Club, whose secretary, Edwin Ash, published an open letter in *The Times* on 4 December 1870 stating: "Those who play the Rugby-type game should meet to form a code of practice, as various clubs play to rules which differ from others, which makes the game difficult to play."

The following month, a meeting of twenty-one London clubs, with Richmond captain E.C. Holmes as chairman, voted to form the Rugby Football Union with Old Rugbeian Algernon Rutter of Richmond FC as its first president.

The joining fee and annual subscription was set at five shillings per club. The twenty-one founder clubs were: Addison, Belsize Park, Blackheath, Civil Service, Clapham Rovers, Flamingoes [*sic*], Gipsies, Guy's Hospital, Harlequins, King's College, Lausanne, Law, Marlborough Nomads, Mohicans, Queen's House, Ravenscourt Park, Richmond, St Paul's School, Wellington College, West Kent and Wimbledon Hornets.

London club Wasps was not represented because its representative went to the wrong venue – legend has it that he went to a pub of the same name but by the time he realised he was too drunk to rectify his mistake.

Along with the Rugby Football Union, a committee was formed to formulate the laws of the game. This task was given to Rutter, Holmes and L.J. Maton, all Old Rugbeians and lawyers, which is why the sport has laws and not rules.

The bulk of the work fell to Maton who was laid up with a broken leg from playing rugby and he used Holmes's chambers. The laws were accepted by the full committee on 22 June 1871, and applied by a Special General Meeting on 24 June. The laws outlawed the practice of hacking and tripping.

FIRST
INTERNATIONAL RUGBY MATCH
FIRST
SCOTSMAN TO PLAY FOR ENGLAND
ONLY
RUGBY INTERNATIONAL INITIATED
BY A LOSS AT SOCCER

**SCOTLAND 1G 1T ENGLAND 1T AT ACADEMY GROUND, RAEBURN
PLACE, EDINBURGH, EH4 SCOTLAND. 3PM MONDAY 27 MARCH 1871.**

In 1870, England beat a London-based Scotland team one-nil in an
Association Football match at the Kennington Oval in London (though
this is not officially recognised; the first official international Association
Football match was a goalless draw between Scotland and England at
The West of Scotland Cricket Ground, Hamilton Crescent, Peel Street,
Partick, Glasgow, Lanarkshire, on 30 November 1872).

The Scots blamed the loss on the fact that the principal code of
football north of the border was rugby and therefore issued a challenge
for what would be the first international rugby match.

Blackheath accepted on behalf of the English (the Rugby Football
Union not yet having been formed, though in the event it was formed a
few weeks before the game was played; see opposite) and twenty players
– thirteen forwards and seven backs, half of them Old Rugbeians – were
selected to meet the Scotland XX in a match of fifty minutes each way.
B.H. Burns of Blackheath became **the first Scot to play for England**
after forward F. S. Isherwood of Oxford University and Ravenscourt
Park failed to show.

Burns is also said to have been an Edinburgh Academical yet his
name cannot be found in the club records of its international players
as one of those who played for another country. In an early example
of gamesmanship, Scotland's pitch was narrow to thwart England's
speedy backs. An estimated four thousand people paid a shilling to
watch Scotland's Angus Buchanan become **the first player to score a try**

in an international, but it did not count for any points. In those days a try was just that – it entitled the team to "try" to convert the touchdown into a goal, which William Cross succeeded in doing for **the only goal of the match**.

But before Cross could take his historic kick there was a ten-minute dispute: Scotland had pushed the scrummage over the line to touch down, a tactic which was then illegal in England. There was no referee but eventually one of the umpires (a role similar to the modern touch judge), Scotsman Doctor H.H. Almond, ruled in favour of his countrymen. Almond later wrote of his decision: "When an umpire is in doubt, I think he is justified in deciding against the side which makes the most noise. They are probably in the wrong."

DID YOU KNOW?

On 30 November 1872, the first football international in the world was watched by around four thousand people at a cricket ground that received £1 10s for its hire.

The match, played in sunshine on a pitch that had been rained on for the previous two days, ended goalless. Scotland's team, clad in "dark blue shirts with a lion crest, white knickerbockers, blue and white striped stockings and red head cowls", was picked by its captain Robert W. Gardener – all of whom played for Queen's Park – and they played in a 2-2-6 formation.

The Football Association picked the England side but Charles Alcock, the Old Harrovian captain of Wanderers, secretary of the FA and creator of the FA Cup, had the most influence. He was unable to play in the inaugural match because of an injury. England, resplendent in "white shirts with three lions crest, white knickerbockers and dark blue caps", played in a 1-2-7 formation.

A report the next day in *Bell's Life in London and Sporting Chronicle* said: "The only thing which saved the Scotch team from defeat, considering the powerful forward play of England, was the magnificent defensive play and tactics shown by their backs, which was also taken advantage of by the forwards…"

FIRST
VARSITY
RUGBY MATCH
OXFORD 1G CAMBRIDGE 0 AT THE PARKS, OXFORD, OX1 3RF
ENGLAND. SATURDAY 10 FEBRUARY 1872.

Of the two ancient universities, **rugby was played first at Cambridge**, when Old Rugbeian Arthur Pell organised a team in 1839 – one former captain recalled games being played on Parker's Piece, where spectators, "from a misapprehension that the players were fighting, rushed on the ground to part the contestants". The Oxford Rugby Football Club was founded at a meeting of Old Rugbeians held in Balliol College on 2 November 1869. Meanwhile, at Cambridge, disputes about rules between footballers from the different public schools led to the formulation, in 1848, of the Cambridge Rules, which would form the basis of Association Football rules when the Football Association was founded in London in October 1863. But rugby purists at Cambridge refused to adopt the Cambridge Rules, and eventually founded the Cambridge Rugby Union Club, under Rugby Football Union rules, in 1872 – the same year as the first Varsity match between the two universities. Of the forty players involved (twenty a side was then standard), twenty-four were Old Rugbeians. Oxford wore dark blue jerseys (the same as today) while the Cambridge team was clad in pink.

ONLY
PLAYER TO CAPTAIN ENGLAND
IN EACH OF HIS TEST MATCHES

Frederic Stokes. England 1t Scotland 1g 1t at Academy Ground, Raeburn Place, Edinburgh, EH4 Scotland. 3pm Monday 27 March 1871. England 2 (1g 1dg 2t) Scotland 1 (1dg) at The Oval, Kennington, Surrey SE11 5SS England. Monday 5 February 1872. England 0 Scotland 0 at Hamilton Crescent, 40-44 Peel Street, Glasgow G11 5LU Scotland. Monday 3 March 1873.

Frederic Stokes played just three times for England and has the unique honour of captaining them on each occasion. He was also one of only three England players to have appeared in every match that England had played by then. He was described as a "brilliant forward, being always on the ball, and often making excellent runs …can also play at capital form at half-back, is a sure tackle and a first-rate drop or place-kick". He retired from international rugby when he was 22. In 1874, he became the second president of the Rugby Football Union and remains the youngest man to have held the position. He died in 1929.

ONLY
PLAYER TO REPRESENT SCOTLAND
AT RUGBY AND FOOTBALL

HENRY RENNY-TAILYOUR. SCOTLAND 1 (1DG) ENGLAND 2 (1G 1DG 2T) (RUGBY) AT THE OVAL, KENNINGTON, SURREY SE11 5SS ENGLAND. MONDAY 5 FEBRUARY 1872. SCOTLAND 2 ENGLAND 4 (FOOTBALL) AT THE OVAL, KENNINGTON, SURREY SE11 5SS ENGLAND. 3PM SATURDAY 8 MARCH 1873.

Henry Waugh Renny-Tailyour was born on 9 October 1849 at Mussoorie, North-Western Provinces, India, where his Scottish father was serving in the Army. The son followed his father into the military and signed for the Royal Engineers. He would rise to the rank of colonel. He was twice chosen to represent Scotland at football and both matches were at Kennington Oval. On 18 November 1871 he captained Scotland in an unofficial match that Scotland lost 2-1; he scored Scotland's solitary goal to make him the first international goalscorer for Scotland. Three months later, he played (also at Kennington Oval) in the oval ball game and was on the losing side as England ran out 2-1 winners. In 1873, he was again chosen for Scotland again at The Oval (where else?) and yet again he as on the losing side although he scored **Scotland's first international goal** as they lost 4-2. Although an outstanding sportsman Renny-Tailyour's selection may have been due to the fact that the Scottish Football Association could only afford return fares for eight players so the remaining three were chosen from London residents. As if playing for Scotland was not enough (also see opposite), Renny-Tailyour was an accomplished cricketer and played first-class cricket for Kent and MCC. He died on 15 June 1920.

DID YOU KNOW?

Having lost the first FA Cup Final in 1872 and again in 1874, the Royal Engineers returned to the final for their third attempt on 13 March 1875, against Old Etonians. The referee was Charles Alcock, the inventor of the FA Cup and captain of the victorious Wanderers team in the first final. Old Etonians won the toss and chose unsurprisingly to play with the wind or, as the newspapers of the time reported it, the "howling gale". Owing to the rule of teams changing ends every time a goal was scored, Royal Engineers played into the wind for all apart from about ten minutes of the game. After thirty-seven minutes Lieutenant Richard Ruck of the Sappers midfield went in for a heavy tackle on Etonian inside-forward Cuthbert Ottaway that resulted in him having to leave the field with an injured ankle. Despite being down to ten men, three minutes later Alexander Bonsor (who had played in the first two finals for Wanderers) curled a corner kick into the goal to give the Old Etonians the lead. The Royal Engineers attacked and scored through Captain Henry Renny-Tailyour. The wind made good play impossible and the match ended one-all after ninety minutes. Thirty minutes of extra time could not break the deadlock and the teams met again three days later at The Oval. Several Old Etonians were unable to make the replay and indeed the team arrived an hour late for the kick-off. Royal Engineers won 2-0 with goals from Lieutenant William Stafford and again from Captain Renny-Tailyour.

LAST

20-A-SIDE RUGBY MATCHES

1874-1875

The game was developing when it was decided to reduce the number of participants on the field. On 13 December 1875, Oxford and Cambridge became the first to reduce their teams from twenty to fifteen-a-side. It had been apparent for some time that the game was becoming less of a spectacle for those watching and merely fun for those playing. On 5 February 1877, the match between England and Ireland held at The Oval was **the first international match between two teams of XV**. England won by two goals and two tries to nil.

FIRST
RECORDED GAME OF RUGBY
ON AMERICAN SOIL
FIRST
GAME OF AMERICAN FOOTBALL

Harvard University 0 McGill University 0 at Jarvis Field, Cambridge, Massachusetts, United States of America. Friday 15 May 1874 and Harvard University 4 Yale University 0 at Hamilton Park, Whalley Avenue and West Park Avenue, New Haven, Connecticut, United States of America. Saturday 13 November 1875.

Until 1874, Harvard played the "Boston Game", a round-ball combination of football and rugby which one 1874 graduate described as "eminently a kicking, as distinguished from a running and tackling, game", although the rules did allow running with the ball. The other Ivy League universities, which had outlawed handling at a meeting in 1873, refused to play the Boston Game, so in 1874 Harvard agreed to a challenge series against Montreal's McGill University – one game of Boston rules (where every game constituted a goal) and one game of rugby. McGill had eleven players and Harvard fifteen so the latter dropped four players to even out the sides. On 14 May, Harvard won the Boston game 3-0 (the first two games lasted about five minutes and the third went to twelve minutes). It was **the first time that an admission fee had been charged for a collegiate sporting event** – the proceeds went on providing lavish food and drink for the McGill team. On 15 May, Harvard struggled to hold McGill to a scoreless draw in the first game of rugby on American soil. But they were hooked; that autumn they beat McGill in Canada, and on 13 November 1875 they persuaded

Yale to play rugby under "Concessionary Rules", arguably the first game of American football. Yale, too, were hooked, and it was Yale's Walter Camp who initiated the rule changes that shaped the sport of American football. Had it not been for Harvard and Yale's enthusiasm for rugby-style football the Ivy League would have continued to play soccer and American football might well have developed as a round-ball game.

FIRST
BROTHERS TO PLAY FOR ENGLAND IN SAME MATCH
REGINALD & LOUIS BIRKETT: ENGLAND 0 SCOTLAND 0 AT ACADEMY GROUND, RAEBURN PLACE, EDINBURGH, EH4 SCOTLAND. MONDAY 8 MARCH 1875

Reginald Halsey Birkett (1849-98) was born at London and was a talented footballer and rugby player. He was one of the thirteen original committee members at the foundation of the Rugby Football Union on 26 January 1871. He played in the first international against Scotland and scored England's first try. He played four times for his country and in the second match he played alongside his brother Louis (1853-1943) who would play for England three times. Reg also played one match for England in goal (against Scotland on 5 April 1879 when England won 5-4) and in 1880 won the FA Cup Final with Clapham Rovers. His son, John (1884-1967), also played rugby for England and was mentioned in dispatches eighteen times in the First World War.

FIRST
INTERNATIONAL PLAYER TO DIE
CHARLES CROMPTON AT BENGAL, INDIA. TUESDAY 6 JULY 1875

Lieutenant-Colonel Charles Arthur Crompton was born at Cork, Ireland on 21 October 1848 and played in the first Test match against Scotland (see 1871), his only appearance for England. He was serving with the Royal Engineers in Bengal when he died, aged 26, from an abscess on the liver.

FIRST

TEST CAPTAIN TO
KILL HIMSELF

GEORGE STACK: IRELAND. THE ROYAL ARCADE
HOTEL, 33 COLLEGE GREEN, DUBLIN, IRELAND.
TUESDAY 14 NOVEMBER 1876.

George Hall Stack captained Ireland in their first international against England in February 1875 at Kennington Oval. He had been instrumental in the organisation of the match and indeed the first meeting of the Irish Football Union was held in Stack's rooms at No 27 Trinity College, Dublin, at 1.30pm on 7 December 1874. The defeat by England was Stack's only appearance for Ireland. In the first nine matches Ireland played, from 1875 to 1882, they had a different captain in each. Less than two years after his solitary cap, 26-year-old bachelor Hall died from an overdose of chloral hydrate. The local paper, *Freeman's Journal and Daily Commercial Advertiser*, reported: "The first witness... Mr Orpen ... had not the slightest doubt that he came to his death by misadventure; witness was aware that some time ago deceased underwent a painful and unsuccessful operation. ... Mr W.T. Kyle, who had lived with the deceased in Trinity College, deposed that he knew he was in the habit of taking opium for the purpose of relieving indigestion; witness often remonstrated with him upon the matter, but deceased had said he suffered very much, and that [witness] had no idea of the pain he suffered. ... Charles H. Hartt, 107 Grafton Street, deposed that he was manager of Messrs. Hamilton and Long's, Grafton Street; deceased was in the habit of taking sedatives, and had an account with witness; he sent the order [produced] on Monday night, and the bottle [produced] was sent to him; the bottle labelled chloral [hydrate] was purchased, witness had no doubt, at his establishment. ... Dr Egan said that from what he had heard of the case he thought it possible that deceased, who he understood had given up opiates, renewed the habit that night, and took as large a dose as he had previously taken without sustaining any injury, but, having for some time ceased to use opiates, he was affected more by what he had taken than had he not for a time relinquished the habit. Four grains was the smallest fatal dose on record; but if the deceased had taken all that was in the smaller bottle he would have swallowed 24 grains. The Coroner briefly reviewed the evidence, and the jury, without hesitation, found that the deceased had come to his death through misadventure."

FIRST
MATCH AT
LANSDOWNE ROAD

LEINSTER BEAT ULSTER AT LANSDOWNE ROAD, BALLSBRIDGE, DUBLIN 4, IRELAND. SATURDAY 16 DECEMBER 1876

Lansdowne Road was created by Henry Wallace Doveton Dunlop (1844-1930), an engineering graduate of Trinity College, Dublin, and the organiser of the first All Ireland Athletics Championships. After a first meeting, the Provost of Trinity told Dunlop to find another venue. Many years later, he remembered: "I was therefore forced to look for another plot, and after careful consideration chose the present Lansdowne Road one. In conjunction with [my] late [trainer] Edward Dillon, I took a 69-year lease from the Pembroke Estate, paying a ground rent of £60 per annum, of part only of the premises stretching from the railway to about sixty yards from the Dodder. I laid down a cinder running path of a quarter-mile, laid down the present Lansdowne Tennis Club ground with my own theodolite, started a Lansdowne archery club, a Lansdowne cricket club, and last, but not least, [in 1872] the Lansdowne Rugby Football Club – colours red, black and yellow." Three hundred cartloads of soil were used to create the pitch. The first match played at the Lansdowne Road stadium was between Leinster XX and Ulster XX with Leinster running out winners. **The first international rugby match played at the stadium** was on 11 March 1878, between Ireland and England who won by a goal, a drop goal and a try. Dunlop charged the Irish Rugby Football Union £5 and half of profits over £50 after expenses. **Ireland's first victory at the ground** took place on 5 February 1887, against England by two goals to nil in the Four Nations Championship. The Irish Rugby Football Union built **the first covered stand** in 1908. It was not until 1974 that the Irish Rugby Football Union bought the freehold of the ground.

FIRST
FULL BACK
H.H. Johnson, Scotland. 1877.

Johnson became the first player to play as a single full back.

DID YOU KNOW?

The 1877 West Wales Challenge Cup Final was between Cardiff and Llanelly and had to be abandoned because the crowd stole the ball.

FIRST
FLY HALF
FIRST
STANDARD THREE-QUARTER LINE
CARDIFF FC, WALES. 1878.

In 1878, Cardiff developed the tactic of giving a short pass to one of the half backs, who would charge headlong with the ball and became known as the flying half back. In 1884, Cardiff became the first club to use the now-standard formation of four three-quarters.

FIRST
RUGBY MATCH
UNDER FLOODLIGHTS
Broughton Rangers 2g 3t Swinton 0 at Yew Street, Salford, Lancashire. M7 2HL England. Tuesday 22 October 1878.

A sudden vogue for floodlit sports events began in the late 1870s as newly founded electric companies sought to prove their superiority over gas, which until then had been the only form of outdoor lighting. Football was first off the mark, with a floodlit game between "Reds" and "Blues" at Sheffield United's Bramall Lane stadium, on 14 October 1878. Four

Siemens arc lamps stood on 30ft wooden towers in each corner of the ground but they were unreliable and it would be almost eighty years before the Football League agreed to their usage in official matches. In front of nearly twenty thousand spectators, John (later Sir Charles) Clegg captained the Reds who beat the Blues, captained by his brother, William Clegg, by two goals to nil. Rugby was only a week behind. The first recorded floodlit rugby match, at Broughton's Yew Street ground, was illuminated by just two Gramme's Lights, each suspended from a 30ft pole. According to the *Salford Weekly News*, "Probably 8,000 to 10,000 persons were present when the time for kick-off arrived" – but they weren't expecting to watch an inter-club match between Broughton Rangers and Swinton. The first floodlit football match attracted a large crowd by inviting guest players to appear (hence the cryptic names of the teams) but the promoters of the rugby match were even more canny: instead of actually paying guest players to appear they simply gave the impression that the match would be between invitation sides, referring to them as Mr A.T. Bowman's XV and Mr W. Longshaw's XV. Bowman and Longshaw were the captains of Broughton Rangers and Swinton respectively, so the marketing was technically correct though not entirely honest. Another match was played in the Liverpool area later that month and on 24 February 1879, **the first floodlit match was played in Scotland** between Hawick and Melrose (Hawick won by a goal to nil). The day before the match a heavy snowstorm struck the area and the pitch was covered with a heavy layer of snow. The club roped in local unemployed men to clear the pitch but a thick frost made conditions dangerous. There was a debate about cancelling the game but by mid-afternoon the electricians had set up the lights, which provided 3,200-candle power. Five thousand people turned up but only £63 was taken at the box office because Hawick did not believe that the match would be popular and hired only one man for the task who sat at a kitchen table with a bowl and a small lamp. Many spectators got in without paying. The match was described as a farce with fans standing on the pitch and in front of the light causing long shadows on the pitch. Players bumped into each other or tried to tackle shadows. As soon as the match was over, the floodlights were switched off causing chaos as the fans tried to leave the ground in the heavy snow.

Note: Contemporary press reports of the first floodlit rugby match refer to other "illuminated matches" but there is no record of any earlier floodlit match other than the Association Football match on 14 October.

DID YOU KNOW?

One reporter of the time did not approve of the new fad, complaining that clubs which used floodlights were attempting to "snuff out the moon".

FIRST

CALCUTTA CUP MATCH

SCOTLAND 1G ENGLAND 1DG AT ACADEMY GROUND, RAEBURN PLACE,
EDINBURGH, EH4 SCOTLAND. MONDAY 10 MARCH 1879.

The Calcutta Cup is played between England and Scotland annually although it derived from a 20-a-side match that was played on 25 December 1872 between England and Scotland, Ireland and Wales in the Indian city. The event was so popular that it was repeated on 1 January 1873. That month the Calcutta Football Club was founded and joined the Rugby Football Union in 1874. However, the climate in India was not especially conducive to playing rugby and when the free bar was abandoned, many of the players lost interest. The members wanted to keep alive the memory of the club and so withdrew the club funds in silver rupees and had them melted down and made into a trophy approximately eighteen inches high. An elephant sits atop the lid and the three handles comprise king cobras. The Calcutta Club presented the trophy to the RFU in 1878 on condition it was played for annually. The club initially wanted a knockout competition along the lines of the FA Cup for English rugby sides. The RFU decided that this went against the spirit of amateurism. The first match ended in a draw. England became the first winners of the Calcutta Cup on 28 February 1880 when they beat the auld enemy by two goals and three tries to one goal at Whalley Range, Manchester.

DID YOU KNOW?

On 5 March 1988, England number eight PC Dean Richards and Scotland's captain flanker John Jeffrey, a farmer, played football with the Calcutta Cup along Princes Street in Edinburgh causing around £1,000 of damage to the valuable trophy. Scotland banned Jeffrey for six months while Richards received only a one-match ban.

FIRST
TRY SCORED BY IRELAND

JOHN LOFTUS CUPPAIDGE: IRELAND 0 (1T) ENGLAND 1 (1G 1T) AT LANSDOWNE ROAD, BALLSBRIDGE, DUBLIN 4, IRELAND. SATURDAY 30 JANUARY 1880.

John Cuppaidge was studying medicine at Trinity College when he scored Ireland's first try in the opening match of the 1879/80 Home Nations. Unfortunately, Robert Walkington missed the conversion and Ireland lost the game. Born on Christmas Day 1856, he played three Tests for Ireland and later set up a medical practice in Queensland. He died on 23 September 1934.

FIRST
MEETING OF THE IRISH RUGBY FOOTBALL UNION

IRISH RUGBY FOOTBALL UNION, 63 GRAFTON STREET, DUBLIN, IRELAND. THURSDAY 5 FEBRUARY 1880.

In the mid-1870s two governing bodies for Irish rugby were formed in the country – the Irish Football Union at Dublin on 12 December 1874 followed the next month at Belfast by the Northern Football Union. Both had responsibility for picking Irish international teams – for Ireland's first match seven were chosen by Dublin, seven by Belfast and the remaining six a selection by both unions. The Irish Football Union finished with twelve players, including nine from Trinity College, but still lost. It took four years before they reached a compromise and agreed to merge the two unions. Dr William Neville was elected as the first president of the Irish Rugby Football Union.

FIRST

ENGLAND TEST APPEARANCE
BY A PLAYER STILL AT SCHOOL

Ryder Richardson: England 2g, 2t Ireland 0 at Whalley Range,
Manchester, Lancashire, M16 England. Saturday 5 February 1881.

William Ryder Richardson was a schoolboy attending Manchester
Grammar School when he was picked for his only Test, which England
won against Ireland.

FIRST

ENGLAND V WALES
INTERNATIONAL

FIRST

OUTING FOR THE
WALES SCARLET JERSEY

ENGLAND 7G 1DG 6T WALES 0 AT MR RICHARDSON'S FIELD
(RECTORY FIELD), CHARLTON ROAD, BLACKHEATH, LONDON SE3
8SR ENGLAND. SATURDAY 19 FEBRUARY 1881.

Wales did not have an auspicious start in international rugby. Having
changed the name of the South Wales Football Union to the Welsh
Football Union in order to secure matches with the other home nations,
the "Father of Welsh Rugby", Richard Mullock, issued an audacious
challenge to England. But Mullock failed to follow it through with
the requisite organisational skills – two of his team didn't receive their
summonses to play, and had to be replaced by two Welsh undergraduates
who had travelled to Blackheath to watch the match. Mullock did
establish one tradition, though – instead of playing in black shirts with a
white leek, as the South Wales Football Club had done, Wales played in
scarlet jerseys adorned with the Prince of Wales feathers. However, pride
in the scarlet jersey wasn't enough to win the day, and Wales went down

by seven goals, one drop goal and six tries to nil (the modern equivalent of 82 points to nil). One Welsh player reportedly commented afterwards: "We were lucky to get nil."

FIRST
WALES INTERNATIONAL VICTORY
FIRST
WALES TRY SCORER

Wales 2g 2t Ireland 0 at Lansdowne Road, Ballsbridge, Dublin 4, Republic of Ireland. Saturday 28 January 1882.

It was in their second outing that Wales recorded their first victory, beating Ireland at their home. Tom Baker Jones of Newport was the first try and points scorer for Wales. Charles Lewis of Llandovery College was **the first Welshman to score with a boot**.

FIRST
DOUBLE INTERNATIONAL PLAYER
AT RUGBY AND CRICKET
FIRST
MAN TO CAPTAIN ENGLAND
AT RUGBY AND CRICKET

A.N. HORNBY, ENGLAND 0 SCOTLAND 2T AT WHALLEY RANGE, MANCHESTER, LANCASHIRE, M16 ENGLAND. SATURDAY 4 MARCH 1882: ENGLAND 101 AND 77 LOST TO AUSTRALIA 63 AND 122 BY SEVEN RUNS AT THE OVAL, KENNINGTON, SURREY SE11 5SS ENGLAND. MONDAY 28-TUESDAY 29 AUGUST 1882.

Albert Neilson, known as "Monkey", Hornby because he was short made his Test debut for England at rugby on 5 February 1877 against Ireland in the first fifteen-a-side international. Coincidentally, the match was played at The Oval. Five years later, he captained England at Manchester against Scotland in the Calcutta Cup who won the match by two tries. He was captain of Lancashire for twenty years but was unable to replicate his county form on the international stage and made just twenty-one runs in his three Tests with an average of 3.50 and a highest score of nine (compared to a top score of 188 for Lancashire) when he opened the second innings with W.G. Grace. He was captain when England lost the only Test of 1882 that led to the Ashes. For a sportsman, he was rather old at 35 when he achieved his feat and it was his last rugby Test. He won nine caps for England at rugby, playing his club rugby for Preston Grasshoppers and Manchester. He also played football for Blackburn Rovers.

FIRST
RUGBY SEVENS TOURNAMENT

MELROSE RFC, THE GREENYARDS, MELROSE, ROXBURGHSHIRE TD6 9SA SCOTLAND. SATURDAY 28 APRIL 1883.

Rugby sevens was the brainchild of a couple of butchers named Ned Haig and David Sanderson, whose club, Melrose RFC, was looking for ways to raise money. Haig suggested a rugby tournament but there was no way of holding several full-scale games in an afternoon so it was decided to reduce the teams to seven players each and the duration of each match to fifteen minutes. The first competition, which began at 12.30pm and finished at 7.30pm, attracted eight teams and as well as the rugby there were foot races, drop kicks, dribbling races and placekicking despite the cold and rather a lot of rain. Special trains were laid on from Galashiels and Hawick and 1,600 tickets were booked. The Galashiels Brass Band provided the crowd with musical relief during the day. The Galashiels spectators could not restrain their enthusiasm and jumping the barriers, encroached onto the field of play several times during matches. Melrose met Gala in the final and the latter were tired having only just seen off St Cuthbert's but had to play on or risk being disqualified. The fifteen went by with both teams failing to break the deadlock and so they agreed to play another fifteen minutes. With five minutes remaining

Melrose's David Sanderson obtained a try and promptly left the field declaring themselves the victors without trying to convert the try. Gala protested claiming that the match was not over. The *Border Advertiser* of 2 May 1883 reported: "The proceedings were then brought to an abrupt conclusion and the spectators left the ground amid much noise and confusion. It is said the referee decided the try in favour of Melrose but that they should have played the quarter of an hour before they were entitled to claim the [Ladies] Cup", which was presented by the ladies of Melrose to "the best team of seven men in any Border Football Club". Haig died on 28 March 1939 at Melrose. Rugby sevens will make its debut in the 2016 Summer Olympics.

FIRST
INTERNATIONAL TEAM TO ASK THE REFEREE TO PENALISE ITS OWN ERROR
FIRST
INTERNATIONAL RUGBY ORGANISATION
ONLY
INTERNATIONAL CANCELLED DUE TO A DROPPED BALL
SCOTLAND: ENGLAND 1G SCOTLAND 1T AT RECTORY FIELD, CHARLTON ROAD, BLACKHEATH, LONDON SE3 8SR ENGLAND. 3.25PM SATURDAY 1 MARCH 1884.

The 1883/84 season saw the first international championship involving all four home nations, the title being decided when England and Scotland, both unbeaten, met at Blackheath in front of some eight thousand spectators. Scotland were leading by an unconverted try when, shortly after half-time, controversy erupted: Scotland's half-back Charles Berry (Fettesian-Lorettonians) knocked the ball backwards, whereupon England's Charles Gurdon (Richmond) collected it and passed it to Richard Kindersley (Oxford University), who took it over the line and touched down. In Scotland, knock backs were illegal, so the Scots insisted the referee should disallow the try and instead award a scrum to England. But knock backs were legal in England, so the English insisted the try should stand, arguing that Scotland should not benefit from their own mistake – a principle not enshrined in the advantage rule until twelve years later. The argument raged for ten minutes until the referee, the ex-Ireland captain George Scriven, ruled in favour of England and Wilfrid Bolton (Blackheath) converted the try to win the championship for England. The Scots were so incensed that they cancelled the following year's fixture, and a year after that Ireland, Scotland and Wales founded the International Rugby Board, stating that the Rugby Football Union was not the sole arbiter of the rules – England refused to join until 1890/91, after being excluded from the international championship in the interim. Never before or since has one fumbled ball had such far-reaching repercussions.

FIRST
RECORDED MENTION OF TRIPLE CROWN
THE IRISH TIMES. SATURDAY 12 MARCH 1884.

The first recorded mention of the Triple Crown occurred in *The Irish Times* in the spring of 1884. "After long years of seemingly hopeless struggle Ireland has achieved the triple crown of rugby honours," wrote the paper's anonymous rugby correspondent. (See 2006.)

FIRST
INTERNATIONAL MATCH AT CARDIFF ARMS PARK
WALES 1DG, 2T IRELAND 0 AT CARDIFF ARMS PARK, WESTGATE STREET, CARDIFF CF10 1JA WALES. SATURDAY 12 APRIL 1884.

Cardiff Arms Park originally played host to cricket in 1848. It was more than twenty years before a rugby ball was kicked there. The name is derived from the hotel, which originally stood on the site in the 17th century. The Arms Park's first stands – holding 300 spectators and costing £50 – opened in 1881. The architect was Archibald Leitch, who had designed Arsenal Stadium, Ibrox and Old Trafford. The first international at Cardiff Arms Park was on 12 April 1884 against Ireland in the Four Nations Championship before five thousand fans. Wales won by a drop goal and two tries to nil and loaned Ireland two players after they turned up short. On 7 October 1966, **the first floodlit game was held at Cardiff Arms Park**, and Cardiff RFC beat the Barbarians by twelve points to eight. The ground remained the home of Wales until 1969/70 when the cricket ground was demolished and Cardiff RFC moved to a new purpose built stadium on the site of the original Cardiff Arms Park. The National Stadium opened on 7 April 1984. It was itself bulldozed in 1997 to make way for the Millennium Stadium when it was discovered it was not big enough (53,000 capacity) to host major events. It was the fourth time Cardiff Arms Park had been developed. By 1999, the Millennium Stadium had replaced the National Stadium/Cardiff Arms Park, as the national stadium of Wales for rugby union and football international matches. Cardiff RFC continued as before to play at Cardiff Arms Park rugby ground. Although the Millennium Stadium is on roughly two-thirds of the National Stadium/Cardiff Arms Park site, it no longer uses the Arms Park name. The official website confuses the issue as well, one section says: "The Millennium Stadium is located on Westgate Street in Cardiff; next to the Cardiff Arms Park", whereas another section specifically refers to the stadium as "The Millennium Stadium, on the Cardiff Arms Park".

FIRST
ABANDONED RUGBY TEST

Ireland v Scotland at Ormeau Park, Ormeau Road, Belfast BT7 3GG Ireland. Saturday 21 February 1885.

In 1892, the Scottish rugby historian R.V. Irvine euphemistically noted: "In 1885, we were without our English fixture (see previous entry), but through a freak in the weather, which interrupted our game with Ireland at Belfast, we unexpectedly had the Irishmen at Raeburn Place on the English date". Scotland, who had been leading by a try to nil when the match was abandoned after thirty minutes, won the replay (held a fortnight later on 7 March in Raeburn Place, Edinburgh) by a goal and two tries. It remained the only abandoned Test match until July 1991 (see 1991). No rugby league Test match has been abandoned although a tour match on 10 July 1954 between New South Wales and an England XIII was called off in the second half when all twenty-six players became involved in a punch-up.

FIRST

REFEREE'S WHISTLE

1885-1886

This was the first season that referees were allocated whistles to help them keep order. It occurred about a dozen years after football referees were given whistles.

ONLY

ONE-ARMED RUGBY PLAYER TO SCORE THIRTEEN

CONVERSIONS OUT OF THIRTEEN

MR WAKEHAM, NEWTON ABBOT V PLYMOUTH. SATURDAY 30 JANUARY 1886.

It is a record that has since been surpassed – scoring thirteen conversions from thirteen attempts but when a player called Wakeham did it towards the end of the nineteenth century, it was claimed as a record for England but his effort had an added specialness – he only had one arm.

DID YOU KNOW?

In 1888 Charles Dickens's son Charles Junior published a London guide entitled *Dickens's Dictionary of London*. The entry for Football states, "Both the Rugby Football Union and the Football Association have their headquarters in London.

"The Union is the stronger body, and under its laws, which permit the ball being carried, quite five times as many matches are played as under the Association laws, which do not allow of the ball being run with. [To the lay mind it is probable that the Association game would be more likely to answer the idea conveyed by the name *foot*-ball. The Rugby game is excellent in its way, but the hand has as much to do with the business as the foot.]"

ONLY

PLAYER TO WEAR A
MONOCLE DURING MATCHES
DOLWAY WALKINGTON: IRELAND 2G ENGLAND 0
AT LANSDOWNE ROAD, BALLSBRIDGE, DUBLIN 4,
IRELAND. SATURDAY 5 FEBRUARY 1887.

Born at Belfast on 25 January 1867, full back Dolway Bell Walkington's brother scored Ireland's first try (see 1880). He won eight caps, captaining his country twice.

However, he is best remembered for wearing a monocle during matches because of his bad eyesight. Before making a tackle he would put the eyeglass in his pocket. He was called "one of the best full backs produced by Ireland before the turn of the century" but only if the sun was out, otherwise "his delicate sight tells terribly against him". He died on 18 April 1926.

FIRST
WALES "HOME" MATCH NOT PLAYED IN WALES

WALES 1T 2DG IRELAND 3T AT BIRKENHEAD PARK, PARK ROAD NORTH, BIRKENHEAD, MERSEYSIDE CH41 8AA ENGLAND. SATURDAY 12 MARCH 1887.

In the 1990s, Wales played their "home" games at Wembley in Middlesex while the Millennium Stadium was constructed. It was not the first time that they played their "home" ties in a foreign country. In the final match of the 1887 Home Nations Championship, they met Ireland at Birkenhead to minimise the travelling costs for the visitors. That was the extent of the Welsh largesse as they inflicted Ireland's second defeat of the tournament on them.

FIRST
"FANTASY RUGBY TEAM"
FIRST
RUGBY TOUR OF AUSTRALIA AND NEW ZEALAND

ANGLO-AUSTRALIAN TOUR THURSDAY 8 MARCH-SUNDAY 11 NOVEMBER 1888.

England had no international fixtures in the season 1887/88 (due to the controversy of 1 March 1884, see page 41) but, absurdly, the Rugby Football Union nonetheless picked a team, all of whose members were awarded caps despite not playing. Several players did have a chance to play international rugby, though, when three professional cricketers, Andrew Stoddart (see opposite), Alfred Shaw and Arthur Shrewsbury, hoping to exploit the enthusiasm shown for cricket tours Down Under, organised an unofficial tour – and one thoroughly disapproved of by the Rugby Football Union. The main bone of contention was the issue of professionalism – Jack Clowes of Halifax was banned from playing for receiving £15 to buy clothing for the tour – an issue commemorated in verse by an anonymous journalist:

> They wished each other luck and wealth
> On Zealand's fruitful ground
> A parrot swinging in a cage
> Joined in the shrill ap plause
> And when it caught a Speaker's rage,
> It cussed the Union's laws.
> "Come drink" cried Paul the Douglas star,
> "Drink to this first of tours;
> The Union raves but still we are…"
> The bird shrieked "AMATEURS!"

For the record, the tourists played fifty-three games, winning twenty-seven of thirty-five rugby matches (with six draws and two defeats) and six of eighteen Australian football matches.

LAST
PLAYER TO CAPTAIN
ENGLAND AT BOTH
CRICKET AND RUGBY
ANDREW STODDART. 1888.

Only two players have captained England at both rugby and cricket. The first was Albert Hornby (see 1882), who might have remained the only one were it not for a freak accident. Bob Seddon was picked as captain of the first tour Down Under (see previous entry) but died aged 28 on tour on 15 August 1888 when his boat capsized while he was sculling on the Hunter River – his feet were caught in the foot straps and he was unable to extricate himself. Stoddart, one of the cricketers who had organised the tour, and was one of two discoverers of the corpse, stepped into the breach as captain. Stoddart played sixteen cricket Tests for England, eight as captain (succeeding W.G. Grace as skipper and becoming the first captain to declare in a Test match) and ten rugby internationals as a three-quarter in addition to the tour, but evidently found it difficult leaving the limelight. He played in **his last cricket Test** on 2 February 1898 against Australia. On Easter Saturday, 3 April, 1915 beset by money worries, in failing health and with an unhappy marriage Stoddart shot himself in the head, aged 52 in a bedroom at his home, 115 Clifton Hill, St John's Wood, Middlesex. Born at 10 Wellington Terrace, Westoe, South Shields, "Stod" did not begin playing cricket until he was 22 in 1885 when he made his debut for Middlesex. He toured Australia four times (twice as captain including a winning tour in 1894/95) and America and West Indies once each. In his fifteen-year career he scored 16,738 first class runs including twenty-six centuries. *Punch* celebrated his crowning glory, captaining England to the Ashes win in 1894/95, with a poem, which contained the lines:

> "Then wrote the queen of England
> Whose hand is blessed by God
> I must do something handsome
> For my dear victorious Stod."

FIRST
WINNERS OF THE
ENGLISH COUNTY CHAMPIONSHIP
YORKSHIRE. JANUARY 1889

The first county match was held in 1870 between Yorkshire and Lancashire at Leeds with the red rose side running out victors by two tries and one goal to nil. Almost twenty years later, the Rugby Football Union sanctioned the first official championship and Yorkshire were declared champions, having beaten their opponents in all six matches. They retained their title the following season after another unbeaten run.

FIRST

TOUR MATCH BY AN OVERSEAS TEAM IN BRITAIN

FIRST

PERFORMANCE OF HAKA

FIRST

INTERNATIONAL BY AN OVERSEAS TEAM IN BRITAIN

FIRST

ENGLAND TEST MATCH

AGAINST NON-NATIONAL OPPONENTS

Surrey 1 Maoris 4 at Richmond, Surrey, England. 3.35pm Wednesday 3
October 1888; England 1g 4t Maoris 0 at Rectory Field, Charlton Road,
Blackheath, London SE3 8SR England. Saturday 16 February 1889.

A year after England's first tour Down Under (see above), a New Zealand
team calling itself the "Maoris" arrived as the first overseas team to tour
Britain, in a mammoth 74-match tour organised by Rugby Football
Union secretary Rowland Hill. The tour included one Test, which
England won easily, though the match was controversial, refereed as
it was by... Rowland Hill. At one stage five of the Maoris left the field
in protest at Hill's decisions, and one contemporary rugby historian
recorded: "The match will be remembered for the rough play and
extraordinary conduct of the Maoris, who during their visit displayed
a remarkable aptitude for disputing the decisions of the officials." The
tour was also memorable for the New Zealanders' distinctive strip. The
first match of the tour was against Surrey at Richmond on 3 October
1888, after which the *Illustrated Sporting and Dramatic News* reported:
"... there is a mixture of the two races, colonial and native... They are
dressed in black knickerbockers and jerseys, which in the case of the

Maoris... gives them a rather sombre aspect; but they are all men of fine growth, well-knit and well proportioned and are all skilled adepts in all points of the game." *The Daily Telegraph* was less than polite informing its readership: "The Maoris have progressed since Captain Cook found the neatly tattooed ancestors of our visitors eating each other in the bush." The Maoris' final record was seventy-eight wins, six draws and twenty-three losses. It was during this tour that the haka was performed. Approximately twelve thousand spectators in south-east London watched the forerunners of the All Blacks as they lost to an England team that fielded a dozen debutants among its fifteen players.

FIRST
WALES INTERNATIONAL TO DIE
Samuel Goldsworthy. Saturday 28 September 1889.

Samuel James Goldsworthy was born at Swansea on 11 February 1855 and made his international debut against Ireland on 12 April 1884, which was **Ireland's first international in Wales**. Wales won the game by a drop goal and two tries to nil. Goldsworthy played two more Tests the following year. He died aged 34.

FIRST
WELSH PLAYER BOUGHT
BY AN ENGLISH CLUB
FIRST
TIME WALES BEAT ENGLAND
FIRST
TEST MATCH HELD AT
CROWN FLATT

WILLIAM JAMES WOOD STADDEN: ENGLAND 0 WALES 1T AT CROWN FLATT, DEWSBURY, WEST YORKSHIRE, ENGLAND. SATURDAY 15 FEBRUARY 1890.

It was seventh time lucky for the Welshmen, having drawn one and lost five of the previous encounters. The match played for the first time at Crown Flatt was England's return to international rugby after two years away. The match was decided by a solitary try from Wales and Dewsbury's William James Wood "Buller" Stadden, whose home ground Crown Flatt was. He had made his international debut six years earlier against Ireland and scored a drop goal. In September 1886, he signed for Dewsbury, becoming the first Welsh player bought by an English club. In all, he played eight international matches for Wales.

DID YOU KNOW?

On Christmas night 1906, Stadden strangled his 37-year-old wife Edith, the mother of his five children, as they lay in bed. The children and a lodger were in the house when Stadden committed the homicide. He tried to slit his own throat and then gave himself up to the police. He died of his injuries on 28 December, aged 45.

FIRST
CAPTAIN OF THE BARBARIANS

ANDREW STODDART: BARBARIANS 9 HARTLEPOOL ROVERS 4 AT HARTLEPOOL, ENGLAND. SATURDAY 27 DECEMBER 1890.

The Barbarians, or Baa Baas, is a rugby team for which players are invited to play. The club was formed at 2am on 9 April 1890 by William Percy "Tottie" Carpmael, in Leuchters Restaurant and later at the Alexandra Hotel in Bradford, where the concept of the Barbarians was agreed. Tottie Carpmael died on 27 December 1936, forty-six years to the day after the Barbarians' first match. The first fixture was eight months later and Andrew Stoddart captained the team. (See above).

> ## DID YOU KNOW?
> Formed in 1890, the Barbarians did not undertake their first international tour until 1957 when they went to Canada.

> ## DID YOU KNOW?
> The Barbarians traditionally wear black and white hooped shirts, black shorts and the stockings of the players' usual club.

ONLY
MAN TO PLAY FOR
TWO NATIONS IN THE
HOME NATIONS CHAMPIONSHIPS

James Marsh, Scotland 2t Wales 0 at Academy Ground, Raeburn Place, Edinburgh, EH4, Scotland. Saturday 2 February 1889 and Scotland 1dg Ireland 0 at Ormeau Park, Ormeau Road, Belfast BT7 3GG Ireland. Saturday 16 February 1889; England 1g 1t Ireland 0 at **Whalley Range, Manchester, Lancashire, M16 England**. *Saturday 6 February 1892.*

James Holt Marsh, who qualified in medicine at Edinburgh University (as did Sir Arthur Conan Doyle), was playing club rugby for the Edinburgh Institute Former Pupils team when he was selected to play for Scotland in the 1889 Home Nations Championship. He made his debut against Wales as a three-quarter. Scotland won and Marsh was chosen for the second and final game of the series against Ireland (England did not compete because of their refusal to join the International Rugby Board). Scotland won and took the champions title although Marsh was never selected again. He moved to Manchester where he ran a GP surgery for forty years and played for Swinton. He was selected to play for England in the match against Ireland at Manchester, again as a three-quarter. England were victorious but once again Marsh was not picked again. Subsequent rule changes mean that he will remain the only person to represent two countries in the Home Nations Championship. He died on 1 August 1928 at Leigh, Lancashire.

FIRST

TIME SCOTLAND WON
THE TRIPLE CROWN

ENGLAND 3 SCOTLAND 9 AT ATHLETIC GROUND, TWICKENHAM ROAD, RICHMOND, SURREY TW9 2SF ENGLAND. SATURDAY 7 MARCH 1891.

The 1891 Home Nations Championship was the ninth series and the fourth time Scotland had won the title but the first occasion they took the Triple Crown. In their opening match on 7 February 1891, they beat Wales 15-0 and then Ireland succumbed 14-0 a fortnight later. Their final match was against the auld enemy and after ten minutes a dropped goal by German-born Paul Clauss (one of the original Barbarians) gave them the lead. Second-half tries from John Orr and Willie Neilson that were both converted by Gregor MacGregor gave the Scots the titles.

FIRST
INTERNATIONAL PLAYED IN
SOUTHERN HEMISPHERE

FIRST
OFFICIAL TRY SCORED BY A
BRITISH ISLES TOURIST

Randolph Aston: British Isles 4 South Africa 0 at Crusaders Ground, Park Drive, Port Elizabeth, 6006, South Africa. Thursday 30 July 1891.

The British Isles' (Lions) tour of 1888 is regarded by purists as unofficial, such was the taint of professionalism. From 9 July to 7 September 1891, the team were invited to South Africa where they played twenty matches and won every one, scoring 226 points and conceding a solitary one on the whole tour. They played three Tests against the Springboks and 6ft

3in, 15-stone Randolph Littleton Aston (1869-1930) of Blackheath and Cambridge University scored the first try in the 4-0 victory. He had a great tour playing in all twenty games including the three Tests and scoring thirty tries in all.

ONLY

TIME A SIDE CONCEDED
NO POINTS IN THE
HOME NATIONS CHAMPIONSHIPS

1892: England 4t 3g Wales 0 at Rectory Field, Charlton Road, Blackheath, London SE3 8SR England. Saturday 2 January 1892; England 1g 1t Ireland 0 at **Whalley Range, Manchester, Lancashire, M16 England**. *Saturday 6 February 1892; Scotland 0 England 1t 1g at Academy Ground, Raeburn Place, Edinburgh, EH4 Scotland. Saturday 5 March 1892.*

Having returned to the Home Nations Championships in 1890 after a two-year gap over their refusal to join the International Rugby Board, England won the Championship (for the fifth time), the Triple Crown (third time) and the Calcutta Cup. For the competition the points scoring system was changed again with a try being upgraded from one point to two, while a goal conversion was increased from two points to three. England did not concede a point, the only occurrence of this feat.

LAST

TIME GOALS COUNTED
FOR MORE THAN TRIES
1893

In 1871, the rules stated that matches would only be decided on the number of goals scored. Four years later, a bid was made (and rejected) that three tries should be equal to one goal. In November of that year the law was modified to "A match shall be decided by a majority of goals, but if the number of goals is equal or no goals be kicked, by a majority of tries." In 1886, a further amendment was made: "A match shall be decided by a majority of points, a goal shall equal three points, and a try one point. If the number of points be equal, or no goal kicked or try obtained, the match shall be drawn. Where a goal is kicked from a try the goal only is scored." In March 1893, the Rugby Football Union and Wales Rugby Union increased the points for a try from two to three points. The conversion was reduced from three points to two, meaning that the value of a converted try stayed at five points. Ireland RFB adopted this scheme the following year.

FIRST

NEW ZEALAND PLAYER SENT OFF

NEW SOUTH WALES 0 NEW ZEALAND XV 16 AT SYDNEY
CRICKET GROUND, MOORE PARK, MOORE PARK
ROAD, SYDNEY, NEW SOUTH WALES 2021 AUSTRALIA.
SATURDAY 29 JULY 1893.

Under the management of G.F.C. Campbell and captained by Thomas Ellison, a 27-man New Zealand touring party arrived in Australia for eleven matches. They won all but one game (against New South Wales 25-3 on 8 July 1893). In the last match, three weeks later, they again clashed with New South Wales before a crowd of twenty thousand spectators. The weather was poor and the ground muddy and sodden. By half-time the tourists were up 7-0 and heading for victory. Towards the end of the match the referee Edward McCausland, a New Zealander who had emigrated to Sydney, stopped the play to speak to William McKenzie, a wing forward who played for Wairarapa. He was nicknamed "Offside Mac" and his tactics did not make him popular. After the referee finished his talk, McKenzie began limping towards the dugout. The crowd believing that McKenzie was injured gave him a respectful round of applause. In fact, McKenzie had become the first Kiwi to be sent off.

ONLY

ENGLAND PLAYER TO
SCORE THREE TRIES AND
FINISH ON LOSING SIDE

**Howard Marshall: England 11 Wales 12 at Cardiff
Arms Park, Westgate Street, Cardiff CF10 1JA Wales.
Saturday 7 January 1893.**

Blackheath fly half Howard Marshall (1870-1929) made his debut in the Five Nations and scored a hat-trick of tries. The match had only just gone ahead as the Arms Park pitch was frozen and was only thawed out when hundreds of braziers were left alight overnight. They left large black circles on the pitch. Despite his barnstorming performance, Marshall was never picked again. It was also in the match that full-back Billy Bancroft scored **the first successful penalty goal in a Test**.

FIRST

TRIPLE CROWN WON BY IRELAND

1894: IRELAND 7 ENGLAND 5 AT RECTORY FIELD, CHARLTON ROAD, BLACKHEATH, LONDON SE3 8SR ENGLAND. SATURDAY 3 FEBRUARY 1894; IRELAND 5 SCOTLAND 0 AT LANSDOWNE ROAD, BALLSBRIDGE, DUBLIN 4, IRELAND. SATURDAY 24 FEBRUARY 1894; IRELAND 3 WALES 0 AT BALLYNAFEIGH, BELFAST. SATURDAY 10 MARCH 1894.

Having beaten England at Blackheath and then Scotland at Lansdowne Road, Ireland moved north to Ballynafeigh where a John Lytle penalty was enough to separate the two teams and give Ireland their first Triple Crown, nineteen years after they began playing international rugby.

FIRST
RUGBY LEAGUE CLUBS

*The Northern Rugby Football Union (NRFU) at George Hotel, St George's Square,
Huddersfield West Yorkshire HD1 1JA England. Thursday 29 August 1895.*

In the late summer of 1895, twenty-two rugby clubs split from the Rugby Football Union to form the Northern Rugby Football Union. Unlike the schism with Association Football, which was about rules and the approach to the game, this split was a class issue. Players in the industrial north could not afford to take time off work to play rugby, and when their clubs adopted the MCC's rules on amateurism, and paid players expenses of six shillings for their missed shifts (known as "broken time" payments), the Rugby Football Union accused them of professionalism. On 20 September 1893, the Rugby Football Union passed a motion outlawing broken time payments and during the next two years twelve Yorkshire clubs resigned from the Rugby Football Union: Batley, Bradford, Brighouse Rangers, Dewsbury, Halifax, Hull, Huddersfield, Hunslet, Leeds, Liversedge, Manningham, and Wakefield Trinity. On 27 August 1895, at the Mitre Hotel, Leeds, these clubs agreed to form a Northern Union, and on 29 August they met nine Lancashire clubs at the George Hotel, Huddersfield, when the Northern Rugby Football Union was officially founded. The first twenty-two rugby league clubs were those above plus: Broughton Rangers, Leigh, Oldham, Rochdale Hornets, St Helens, Tyldesley, Warrington, Widnes and Wigan; despite no representative being present, Stockport was also included, having been represented by telephone. Dewsbury withdrew shortly afterwards and was replaced by Runcorn; so twenty-two clubs began the first Northern Rugby Football Union season despite this early withdrawal. Many historians consider the Rugby Football Union's refusal to allow broken time payments to be motivated purely by class – to make rugby the preserve of "gentlemen" rather than workers – particularly given that one England captain, Albert Hornby (see 1882) noted, "the so-called amateur sides… distribute expenses far larger than would be paid to a professional player". Whatever the truth, the northerners noted with satisfaction that due to the absence of so many of its best players it was nearly eighteen years after the schism before England regained the rugby union international championship. The organisation changed its name to the Rugby Football League in June 1922. The sixty-bedroom George Hotel, built in 1851, closed in January 2013.

FIRST
RUGBY LEAGUE CHAMPIONS

MANNINGHAM, VALLEY PARADE, BRADFORD, WEST YORKSHIRE BD8 7DY ENGLAND. SATURDAY 25 APRIL 1896.

Even before the schism (see 1895), the northern clubs had defied the Rugby Football Union by organising league competitions in the form of the Yorkshire Senior Competition and the Lancashire Club Championship – the first winners, in the season 1892/93, were Bradford and Oldham respectively. In 1895/96, the first season after the split, all twenty-two Northern Rugby Football Union clubs played each other in a competition known as The Northern Rugby Football League. On the final day of the season two clubs were in contention: league leaders Manningham (based in Bradford), and Halifax, who could win the title if they won and Manningham lost. As the Halifax game ended in an 8-0 victory over Warrington, Manningham were drawing 0-0 with Hunslet and a play-off seemed inevitable. Then Manningham centre Jack Brown attempted a drop-goal (then worth four points). It hit the post and then wobbled over the bar to give Manningham victory and the first NRFU championship title. They played forty-two games, winning thirty-three and losing nine.

DID YOU KNOW?

Despite this early success rugby league did not prosper for long in Manningham. The club's finances became so dire that in 1903 they had to organise an archery competition to raise money, after which the club was persuaded to convert to Association Football, and on 29 May 1903 began a new life as Bradford City even though they had never played a game of football.

FIRST

WINNERS OF RUGBY LEAGUE
CHALLENGE CUP

FIRST

PLAYER TO SCORE IN A
CHALLENGE CUP FINAL

FIRST

TRY-SCORER IN A
CHALLENGE CUP FINAL

ONLY

CHALLENGE CUP
FINAL IN WHICH A DROP-GOAL
SCORED 4 POINTS

Batley 10 St Helens 3 at Headingley, Leeds, West Yorkshire LS6 3BU
England. 3pm Saturday 24 April 1897.

The rugby league Challenge Cup – inaugurated as the NRFU Challenge
Cup – is the sport's most respected and glamorous knockout trophy. The
three-feet high cup was made by Fattorini & Sons of Bradford (who later
made the current FA Cup) at a cost of £60, and the first ties, involving
fifty-two clubs (though twelve had byes), were played on 20 March 1897.
Five weeks later, 13,492 people flocked to Headingley to pay £624 17s 7d
to watch the final, which the *Leeds Mercury* described as: "A big success,
financially, socially, and from a football point of view." The final was not
a sell-out; indeed the ground was only about 65 per cent full. Before the
match the new cup was paraded through the streets in a procession of
horse-drawn carriages, which stopped at the Mitre Hotel to pick up the
Batley team en route to Headingley. Batley scored a difficult drop-goal
after just five minutes, reputedly causing one young spectator to fall out
of a tree in excitement – fly-half J Oakland thus became **the first player
to score in a Challenge Cup Final**, and soon afterwards captain John
Goodall became **the first try-scorer**, giving Batley a 7-0 lead at half-

time. A try apiece in the second half made Batley the first holders of this most cherished of trophies, which was celebrated in unusual fashion by a 160-gun salute made up of railway fog signals which detonated one by one as the team train passed over them on the way back to Batley. Batley Old Band then escorted them to the town hall. St Helens made amends a hundred years later by becoming the centenary winners, beating Bradford Bulls 32-22 at Wembley on 2 May 1997.

LAST
RUGBY LEAGUE LINEOUT
NRFU, 1897/98

As well as being the only Challenge Cup final in which a drop-goal would count for four points, Batley's win (previous entry) was also the only final to involve lineouts. The first of the rule changes that would shape the game of rugby league were made on 9 December 1895, the first season of the split, and included penalties for a deliberate knock-on and for half-backs who did not stand behind the rearmost forward at scrums. But the first change that made the game look significantly different from rugby union was the abolition of the lineout, which was replaced by a punt-in from touch for the 1897/98 season (in 1902 the punt-in was replaced by a scrum ten yards in from touch). That season it was also decided that all goals would count for two points.

FIRST
BROTHERS TO SCORE
TRIES FOR ENGLAND
IN SAME MATCH
Percy and Frank Stout: England 14 Wales 7 at Rectory Field, Charlton Road, Blackheath, London SE3 8SR England. Saturday 2 April 1898

The Stout brothers were the first brothers to score tries in the same international match for England. Percy Wyfold Stout DSO, OBE (1875-1937) played football before switching to rugby and represented his country five times, scoring his only international try in the same match that brother Frank scored. It would be the last time the feat would be achieved until 1993 when Rory and Tony Underwood scored in the 1993 Five Nations Championship. His rugby career over, Percy Stout emigrated to Cairo where he became a stockbroker. In the First World War, he was mentioned in dispatches five times and awarded the Distinguished Service Order in 1917. Younger brother Frank Moxon Stout (1877-1926) was more successful, playing fourteen times for England and seven times for the British Isles (Lions), at times captaining both sides (see below). In the First World War, he was awarded the Military Cross.

ONLY
MAN TO CAPTAIN AND COACH
BRITISH LIONS ON SAME TOUR

REVEREND MATTHEW MULLINEUX MC: BRITISH ISLES (LIONS) TO AUSTRALIA. WEDNESDAY 14 JUNE-SATURDAY 19 AUGUST 1899.

Reverend Matthew Mullineux (1867-1945) made his Test debut on the previous tour against South Africa and was instrumental in arranging the 1899 tour, appointing himself to the plum roles of captain and coach. He only played in the first Test, surrendering the captaincy to Frank Stout (see previous entry). Mullineux became a chaplain in the Army, and was awarded the Military Cross for his gallantry during the First World War.

FIRST
WELSH RUGBY UNION PLAYER
TO WIN A BRITISH ISLES (LIONS) CAP

GWYN NICHOLLS, BRITISH LIONS 3 AUSTRALIA 13 AT SYDNEY CRICKET GROUND, MOORE PARK, MOORE PARK ROAD, SYDNEY, NEW SOUTH WALES 2021 AUSTRALIA. SATURDAY 24 JUNE 1899.

Three-quarter Erith Gwyn Nicholls (who was actually born at Westbury-on-Severn in England) made his debut for Wales on 25 January 1896 at

Cardiff Arms Park in a victory against Scotland. His international career was put on hold for a year because of the Gould Affair, when Wales withdrew from Test matches because of allegations of professionalism when a testimonial was arranged for Arthur Gould. Nicholls won twenty-four caps for Wales between 1896 and 1906 including ten as captain. In 1899, he became the first Welshman to be selected for the British Isles when he was chosen to tour Australia.

The party – the first to truly represent all four countries – set off from Charing Cross Station on 9 May 1899 on a journey that took five weeks before they arrived Down Under on 11 June.

The team played twenty-one matches including four Tests. They won their first three warm-up games in Australia before losing **the first Test in Australia** 13-3. The captain and manager Reverend Matthew Mullineux responded by dropping himself for the rest of the series.

DID YOU KNOW?

Gwyn Nicholls was originally registered on his birth certificate as Edith Gywn Nicholls.

Mullineux is **the only player to represent the British Isles without playing for his country**.

Frank Stout took over the captaincy (see above) and Charles Adamson took Mullineux's place in the side. The Lions won the remaining three Tests – 11-0 (at Brisbane on 22 July 1899), 11-10 (at Sydney on 5 August 1899) and 13-0 (also at Sydney, a week later on 12 August 1899) – and Nicholls, known as "The Prince of Three-quarters", was the undoubted star of the series.

He finished the tour as top try scorer with ten to his name and also claimed a then Lions record for the fourth Test scoring ten points. On Boxing Day 1949, his team-mate Rhys Gabe officially opened the Gwyn Nicholls Memorial Gates at Cardiff Arms Park.

On 16 November 2005, Nicholls was inducted into the International Rugby Hall of Fame.

FIRST

RUGBY UNION INTERNATIONAL
TO WIN THE VICTORIA CROSS

Captain Robert Johnston at the Battle of Elandslaagte, Boer War,
Natal, South Africa. Saturday 21 October 1899.

Only four rugby union internationals have won the VC, three of them
from the Irish Wanderers club. The first was Johnston, who remained
in South Africa after touring with England-Ireland and winning the
1896 Test series against the Springboks. He later captained Transvaal to
a Currie Cup victory and in 1898, with the Boer War imminent, joined
the Imperial Light Horse (Natal), South African Forces. The 27-year-old
captain won his VC at the Battle of Elandslaagte, near Ladysmith – when
his troops' advance was halted by heavy fire at point-blank range Johnston
and Captain Charles Mullins (also to be awarded with the VC) charged
forward, renewing the momentum of the advance and enabling a decisive
flanking movement to go ahead. The wounded Johnston was nursed
by rugby's second VC-winner, Surgeon Captain (later Major) Thomas
Crean, a star forward who had travelled to South Africa on the same tour.
Crean won his VC two years later, on 18 December 1901 at Tygerkloof
Spruit, for continuing to attend to the wounded, under heavy fire from
only 150 yards, despite being injured himself. A third Irish rugby union
international, Lieutenant (later Brigadier) Frederick Harvey, won a VC
on 27 March 1917 at Guyencourt, France, for single-handedly capturing
a machine gun. (See also 1918.)

ONLY

SCOTTISH INTERNATIONAL KILLED IN THE BOER WAR

DOUGLAS MONYPENNY AT BATTLE OF PAARDEBERG, BOER WAR,
PAARDEBERG DRIFT, ORANGE FREE STATE, SOUTH AFRICA.
THURSDAY 22 FEBRUARY 1900

Douglas Blackwell Monypenny was capped three times for Scotland in
the 1899 Home Nations Championship. He played for London Scottish.
He was the only Scottish Test player to die in either Boer War. He was
21. Two British soldiers were awarded posthumous Victoria Crosses as a
result of their actions at the battle.

FIRST

ENGLAND INTERNATIONAL TO BECOME AN MP

Arthur Heath, Hanley (Conservative). Thursday 4 October 1900.

Arthur Howard Heath was born on 29 May 1856 at Newcastle-under-Lyme in Staffordshire and educated at Clifton College and Brasenose College, Oxford. As well as rugby, he was a skilful cricketer making forty-four first class appearances. He played in the last twenty-a-side international in 1876. In July 1892 and 1895, he unsuccessfully contested the constituency of Hanley in Staffordshire before finally being returned on 4 October 1900. He lost his seat in the 1906 General Election to the Liberals. In January 1910, he won the Leek division of Staffordshire, with a majority of only ten but did not contest the seat in the December election. He died aged 73 on 24 April 1930 at Marylebone, London.

FIRST

RUGBY LEAGUE CLUB TO WIN THE DOUBLE

FIRST

PLAYER TO SCORE A CHALLENGE CUP FINAL HAT-TRICK

BOB WILSON: BROUGHTON RANGERS, BROUGHTON, SALFORD, ENGLAND. CIRCA 4PM SATURDAY 26 APRIL 1902.

Broughton Rangers, who played in **the first rugby match under floodlights** (see 1878), were also the first club to win the double of Rugby League Championship and Challenge Cup in the same season. On 14

April 1902, the last day of the league season, they beat Runcorn 10-0 to complete a record of: W21, L4, D1. Twelve days later they appeared in the final of the Challenge Cup at the Athletic Ground, Rochdale, ready to make history – and they did it in high-scoring style, beating Salford 25 points to nil, which remained the Challenge Cup's highest winning margin until 1915. Salford arrived late and kick-off was delayed by nearly an hour until just before 4pm – and when the game ended about an hour and a half later, Broughton became the first club to win the double, their captain Bob Wilson having dominated the game and become the first man to score a hat-trick in a Challenge Cup Final. One newspaper wrote, "The Broughton skipper is not merely a sprinter. In tackling, marking, and defensive play he is equally at home. Really in the first half it was Salford v Wilson." In 1946/47 the club changed its name to Belle Vue Rangers and although they twice were runners-up in the Lancashire Cup (1946/47 and 1947/48) the good times were over and the club went out of business in 1955. (See also 1996)

FIRST
RUGBY UNION TEST SERIES
WON BY SOUTH AFRICA
ONLY
RUGBY FOOTBALL TEST MATCH
IN WHICH BOTH CAPTAINS
AND THE REFEREE WERE
SCOTTISH INTERNATIONALS
SOUTH AFRICA 10 BRITISH ISLES 10 AT OLD WANDERERS, JOHANNESBURG, GAUTENG, SOUTH AFRICA. WEDNESDAY 26 AUGUST 1903.

The first Test of the 1903 tour was the only occasion in either code of rugby over which Scotsmen had such a wide-ranging influence. The Britain Isles captain was farmer Mark Morrison, who captained Scotland fifteen times, including leading them to Triple Crowns in 1901 and 1903.

One of Morrison's team in the 1901 victory was Alex Frew, a doctor who had since emigrated to the Transvaal and now stood opposite him as captain of South Africa. Four years earlier the referee, iron merchant Bill Donaldson, had been **the first Scotsman to score on Scotland's new national ground at Inverleith**, Edinburgh. The first two Tests of the tour were drawn and South Africa, who would not lose a series at home for more than half a century, won their first Test series with victory in the third.

FIRST
FATHER AND SON TO PLAY
FOR ENGLAND

WILLIAM MILTON: ENGLAND 1G SCOTLAND 0 AT THE OVAL, KENNINGTON, SURREY SE11 5SS ENGLAND. MONDAY 23 FEBRUARY 1874; "JUMBO" MILTON: ENGLAND 14 WALES 14 AT WELFORD ROAD STADIUM, AYLESTONE ROAD, LEICESTER LE2 7TR ENGLAND. SATURDAY 9 JANUARY 1904.

Sir William Henry Milton, KCMG, KCVO (1854-1930) had a varied career. He was the third administrator of Mashonaland, played rugby for England and was the second man to captain South Africa's Test cricket side. Born at Little Marlow, Buckinghamshire, he played twice for England (in 1874 and 1875) when the sport was still a twenty-a-side game. In 1878, he emigrated to South Africa where, on 12 March 1889, he played in South Africa's first Test, which England won by eight wickets. Milton scored one and nineteen and took one for five in England's first innings. In 1901, he became administrator of the whole of Southern Rhodesia, a position he held until 1 November 1914.

He had three sons, Henry Cecil (1884-1961), John Griffin (1885-1915), known as Jumbo, who both played rugby for England, and Noel, who played for Oxford University. Jumbo was at school when he was called up to play for England. He played in all three Home Nations Championship Tests in 1904.

FIRST
INTERNATIONAL
RUGBY LEAGUE MATCH
ONLY
12-A-SIDE RUGBY LEAGUE
TEST MATCH

**ENGLAND 3 OTHER NATIONALITIES 9 AT CENTRAL PARK,
CENTRAL PARK WAY, WIGAN, LANCASHIRE WN1 1XS ENGLAND.
TUESDAY 5 APRIL 1904.**

The first rugby league "international" was played between England and
Other Nationalities (mostly Welsh and Scotsmen) at Central Park in
1904. Other Nationalities won 9-3 in the experimental loose forward-
less twelve-a-side game, with Wigan players David "Dai" Harris, and
Eli Davies in the Other Nationalities team. In fact, England actually
began with eleven players on the pitch as James Lomas arrived late.
Central Park, which opened in 1902, closed in 1999, the same year it was
demolished. The **final game at Central Park was on 5 September 1999**
and Wigan beat St Helens by 28-20, 96 years and 364 days after the first
game against Batley was played. It is now a Tesco car park.

FIRST
BRITISH TOURING PLAYER
SENT OFF

Denys Dobson: British Isles XV 17 Northern Districts 3 at Newcastle,
New South Wales, Australia. Wednesday 6 July 1904.

Oxford-educated Denys Dobson played six Tests for England and was
also chosen for the four-Test British Isles tour of Australia and New
Zealand, led by Darkie Bedell-Sivright. The sixth match of the tour
was against the Northern Districts, four days after the first Australia

Test, which the tourists had won. In the second half, Harry Dolan, the referee, awarded the Northern Districts team a free-kick at a scrum. Dobson took umbrage and let forth with some invective at the official to which Dolan took objection. Dolan sent Dobson from the pitch and Bedell-Sivright led his team off in protest. After twenty minutes' deliberation, the British Isles returned to the pitch, without Dobson. An inquiry was launched by the New South Wales Rugby Union and five of the Australian team supported the referee's version of events while British Isles players Swannell and Bush along with Dobson disputed the allegation. The inquiry report issued in August 1904 exonerated Dobson, described by Darkie Bedell-Sivright as "one of the quietest and most gentlemanly members of the team", said that "the indecent expression reported by the referee was not used by Mr Dobson" and the "crime" was downgraded from "indecent language" to using "an improper expression". (See 1916.)

FIRST
ALL-TICKET TEST MATCH
ONLY
INTERNATIONAL TEAM IRELAND HAVE PLAYED AND NEVER BEATEN

NEW ZEALAND: IRELAND 0 NEW ZEALAND 15 AT LANSDOWNE ROAD, BALLSBRIDGE, DUBLIN 4, IRELAND. SATURDAY 25 NOVEMBER 1905.

The first All Blacks team to visit Dublin created such interest that the Irish Rugby Football Union made the match the first all-ticket rugby international. The visitors ran out convincing winners. Up to 2013, Ireland have met the All Blacks twenty-eight times and have never won a match from the first time in 1905. Some of the matches have been very one-sided affairs: 43-19 in 1995, 63-15 in 1997, 40-8 in 2002, 47-5 in 2005, 66-28 in 2010 and 60-0 in 2012.

FIRST
WINNERS OF RUGBY LEAGUE
COUNTY CUPS

YORKSHIRE: HUNSLET 13 HALIFAX 3 AT PARK AVENUE CRICKET GROUND, HORTON PARK AVENUE, BRADFORD, WEST YORKSHIRE, ENGLAND. SATURDAY 2 DECEMBER 1905; LANCASHIRE: WIGAN 8 LEIGH 0 IN A REPLAY AT WHEATER'S FIELD, BROUGHTON, SALFORD, LANCASHIRE, ENGLAND. MONDAY 11 DECEMBER 1905.

The two County Cups were inaugurated in the same season, 1905/06. The Yorkshire County Rugby Football Challenge Cup got under way on 16 September 1905 with a preliminary round tie between Featherstone Rovers and Huddersfield, and The Lancashire County Rugby Football Challenge Cup began four weeks later, the first round being played on 14 October. The two finals were played on the same day, 2 December: Wigan and Leigh drew 0-0 in front of 16,000 spectators in the Lancashire Cup and Halifax defeated Hunslet in front of 18,500 in the Yorkshire Cup. Wigan emerged as inaugural winners of the Lancashire Cup after a replay on 11 December – they were also the last winners of the Lancashire Cup. (See 1993).

FIRST
RUGBY UNION ALL BLACKS
TOUR OF BRITAIN
FIRST
TEAM TO BEAT THE
ALL BLACKS ON BRITISH SOIL
FIRST
INTERNATIONAL RUGBY UNION
SIDES TO ADOPT NUMBERED SHIRTS

LAST
INTERNATIONAL RUGBY UNION
SIDE TO ADOPT NUMBERED SHIRTS

Wales 3 New Zealand 0 at Cardiff Arms Park, Westgate Street, Cardiff CF10 1JA Wales. Saturday 16 December 1905.

The first All Blacks side – known as the Originals – toured the British Isles, France and the United States of America in 1905/06, arriving in England on 8 September. They played their first match against Devon at Exeter on 16 September 1905 and won convincingly 55-4 before a crowd of six thousand. Billy Wallace scored twenty-eight points, including three tries, and it would be another fifty-one years before another All Black would score more points in a match. The next day the local paper *The Express and Echo* reported: "The All Blacks, as they are styled by reason of their sable and unrelieved costume, were under the guidance of the captain (Mr Gallaher) and their fine physiques favourably impressed the spectators." Four days later, the Kiwis met Cornwall at the Recreation Ground in Camborne. The All Blacks ran out 41-0 victors. They beat every English side that they faced. On 18 November, they beat Scotland 12-7; a week later, they put Ireland to the sword 15-0 and on 2 December they beat England by the same score. Then came a visit to the Arms Park in Cardiff where they lost their only match of the tour. Forty-seven thousand spectators watched the Test, which was controversial before it even began. The two sides could not agree on a referee. George Dixon, the All Blacks' manager, rejected all of the suggestions made by the Welsh Rugby Union and his suggestions were turned down by the WRU. Finally, they settled on John Dallas, a Scotsman, but he was not a success. He was criticised for the kit he wore, deemed unsuitable for a referee, and his inability to keep up with the play. The All Blacks were penalised so often in the scrum (they had only two up front) that their captain ordered the team not to contest them and let the Welsh side win. Wales finally managed to score in the first half but missed the conversion and despite the All Blacks putting Wales under pressure they could not score and the match ended at 3-0. After beating Swansea on 30 December, they travelled to France where they beat the national side on New Year's Day and then went to California. The 1905 All Blacks tour of Britain went on to achieve legendary status within the rugby world and New Zealand in particular. They scored 976 points and conceded only 59, and thus set the standard for all subsequent All Black sides. The tour also saw the first use of the All Blacks name and established New Zealand's reputation as a world-class rugby nation. Some of these players eventually defected to participate in the professional 1907/08 tour of Australia and Great Britain where they played against Northern Union sides in the sport that would eventually become known as rugby league. Although programmes listing teams had been around since the 1870s it was still difficult for some spectators to identify certain players. When Queensland met New Zealand in Brisbane in 1897 it was the **first time anywhere in the world that players wore numbers**. The first international in which teams wore numbers was the Wales-All Blacks clash in 1905 although it would not be until 21 January 1922 when England came to the Arms Park that both sides in the Five Nations wore numbered shirts. Scotland was the last team to adopt numbers on their shirts. When they played England at Twickenham in 1924 and King George V asked J. Aikman Smith, the president of the Scottish Rugby Union, why his players did not sport numbers he replied, "This is a rugby match, not a cattle market."

ONLY
POLICEMAN TO FORCE A
CHANGE IN THE LAWS

WALES 9 (3T) SCOTLAND 3 (1G) AT CARDIFF ARMS PARK, WESTGATE STREET, CARDIFF CF10 1JA WALES. SATURDAY 3 FEBRUARY 1906.

It is fair to say that from 1900 until 1909 Wales and Scotland dominated the Home International Championships. For the 1906 encounter before 25,000 spectators, the Chief Constable of Cardiff wanted to oversee his men so spent the whole match patrolling the touchline in his full dress uniform. Scottish legend Darkie Bedell-Sivright had the Wales posts in sight and charged towards them for what appeared to be a definite try when the ball hit the patrolling policeman and although it bounced back into Bedell-Sivright's arms, it was declared no try. As a result the law was changed so that if any fan was in the home in-goal area they should be considered "in play".

ONLY

MAN WHO PLAYED
TEST RUGBY AFTER
REFEREEING A TEST MATCH

VINCENT CARTWRIGHT: IRELAND 6 SCOTLAND 13 AT LANSDOWNE ROAD, BALLSBRIDGE, DUBLIN 4 IRELAND. SATURDAY 24 FEBRUARY 1906

Vincent Cartwright made his Test debut for England against Wales at Swansea on 10 January 1903 in a match England lost 21-5. He played fourteen times in all for England including captaining his country in all four matches of the 1906 Five Nations. On 10 February, he skippered England as they lost to Ireland 16-6 at Welford Road, Leicester. A fortnight later, he was again on the same pitch as the Irish but this time he was the man in black officiating at the match at Lansdowne Road. On St Patrick's Day, he was back in his England kit as his side beat Scotland 9-3 (see below).

FIRST

BLACK MAN
TO PLAY RUGBY UNION
FOR ENGLAND

JAMES PETERS: ENGLAND 9 SCOTLAND 3 AT INVERLEITH, SCOTLAND. SATURDAY 17 MARCH 1906.

James Peters was born on 7 August 1879 at 38 Queen Street, Salford, Lancashire. His upbringing was unusual – his Jamaican father was mauled to death by lions and his mother from Shropshire, unable to cope, left him with the circus.

Under the big top, he was a bareback horse rider until, aged 11, he broke his arm and the circus abandoned him. He was taken in by an orphanage and showed a sporting prowess that led to him playing for Bristol Rugby Club. On St Patrick's Day 1906, he made his first appearance for England in a victory over Scotland. He was known as "Darkie" Peters and, as *The Yorkshire Post* reported, "his selection is by no means popular on racial grounds" while *The Sportsman* opined that the "dusky Plymouth man did many good things, especially in passing". He went on to win four more caps for England but on 17 October 1906 was at the centre of a racial storm when the touring South African side refused to play his team Devon if Peters was included.

Twenty thousand people turned up at the Plymouth County Ground to watch and it took the combined efforts of the South African High Commissioner and local dignitaries to persuade the Springboks to play. Furious, they agreed and ran out 22-6 winners. Six weeks later, he was dropped from the Test side because of the colour of his skin. In 1909, a dockyard accident cost him three fingers. The next black player to appear for England was wing Chris Oti, eighty-two years later. Peters died on 26 March 1954.

LAST
15-A-SIDE RUGBY LEAGUE MATCH
LAST
RUGBY LEAGUE MATCH TO FEATURE RUCKS AND MAULS
ONLY
MAJOR SPORT WITH 13 PLAYERS A SIDE

BRADFORD NORTHERN 5 SALFORD 0, CHALLENGE CUP FINAL AT HEADINGLEY, LEEDS, WEST YORKSHIRE LS6 3BU ENGLAND. SATURDAY 28 APRIL 1906.

A defining feature of rugby league is that there are thirteen players on a team. Indeed, in France (where the sport was banned during the Second

World War by the Vichy government) it was launched in 1934 as jeu à treize: "the game of thirteen". But it was not always so: rugby league followed rugby union practice of fifteen-a-side until 12 June 1906, when (after a proposal for twelve-a-side was rejected) teams were officially reduced to thirteen-a-side to encourage more open play. It was also on this day that another defining feature entered the rulebook: the play-the-ball rule was introduced, which meant that rucks and mauls (in which spectators could not see the ball) were replaced by a quick, clean restart after a tackle. The last fifteen-a-side rugby league matches, and the last to feature rucks and mauls, were played on 28 April 1906. Some league matches were played on that day (including champions Leigh's 0-0 draw at Barrow) but the most prominent match was Bradford's Challenge Cup Final victory over Salford, played in rain, sleet and gale force winds. Afterwards Bradford's George Marsden said, "I don't think the way we have played a team in the Union could beat us."

━━•◆•◆••◆•━━

LAST
RUGBY LEAGUE CLUB
TO LOSE EVERY FIXTURE IN A SEASON

ONLY
FIRST CLASS RUGBY LEAGUE CLUB
TO LOSE EVERY FIXTURE
IN THE CLUB'S HISTORY

Liverpool City and Runcorn Highfield. 1906/07 and 1989/90.

The first incarnation of Liverpool City rugby league club disbanded after just one season – and in that season they lost thirty out of thirty-two league matches and both their cup-ties. The other two league games were both expunged from the record because the return fixtures weren't played. One of the expunged results was a loss to Pontefract, who withdrew from the league after eight matches, and the other would have saved Liverpool

City from the ignominy of losing every fixture in the club's history: it was a draw with Bramley.

The second and last club to lose all its fixtures in a season was Runcorn Highfield, which in 1989/90 lost all twenty-eight of their league matches and all three cup-ties. Ironically, one of Runcorn Highfield's eight incarnations was as... Liverpool City. (See 1933/34).

DID YOU KNOW?

One first class club has had an even longer losing run than either Liverpool City (thirty-two games) or Runcorn Highfield (thirty-one games) – between November 1975 and April 1977, Doncaster lost thirty-seven consecutive league and cup matches.

ONLY

SCOTSMAN TO WIN
THREE TRIPLE CROWNS
DARKIE BEDELL-SIVRIGHT FOR SCOTLAND.
1901, 1903, 1907.

Scottish legend Darkie Bedell-Sivright is regarded as the most talented forward of his generation and was educated at Fettes (the same school attended by James Bond and Tony Blair). He made his international debut on 27 January 1900 against Wales at St Helen's, Swansea, in which the home side won 12-3. Bedell-Sivright went on to win twenty-two caps for his country. A medical graduate, he was commissioned as a surgeon in the Royal Navy on 25 January 1915. He was posted to Gallipoli during the Dardanelles Campaign in May that year. While serving in the trenches he was bitten by an insect, and on 5 September he died of septicaemia. He was 34.

ONLY
WELSHMAN TO PLAY IN
WINNING WELSH RUGBY UNION
AND LEAGUE TEAMS
AGAINST NEW ZEALAND

**Dai "Tarw" Jones, Wales 3 "The Original" All Blacks
0 at Cardiff Arms Park, Westgate Street, Cardiff CF10
1JA Wales. Saturday 16 December 1905 and Wales 9
New Zealand "All Golds" 8 at Aberdare Athletic Ground,
Aberdare, Wales. Wednesday 1 January 1908.**

David Jones – known as Tarw (Welsh for bull) – was born in 1881 at Tynewydd, a small village in the Rhondda Valley. After starting life as a collier he then became a policeman before returning to the pit. He was rather hotheaded, once throwing an inspector out of his own station and Jones was disciplined for selling raffle tickets in uniform on duty.

On 11 January 1902, he made his debut for Wales against England at Blackheath in a match that Wales narrowly won 9-8. Three years later, he was selected for his country to play against "The Original" All Blacks.

The Kiwis were unbeaten in their previous twenty-seven matches on the tour, their first. Wales, unbeaten in the previous year and Triple Crown holders, went into the match optimistically and that was repaid when they won 3-0. On 1 December 1906 at Swansea, against South Africa Jones played in his thirteenth and last rugby union Test. The following year, he was banned from rugby union for life in a row over payment, then against the rules. He signed for Merthyr Tydfil RLFC and played against the All Golds on New Year's Day 1908. Jones was the northern hemisphere's second dual-code rugby international, just three years after fellow Rhondda player Jack Rhapps – although Rhapps was not on the winning side on both occasions. He retired not long after and became a publican. He was wounded fighting at the Somme (1916) and died in 1933.

FIRST
RUGBY LEAGUE TEST MATCH
FIRST
OVERSEAS RUGBY LEAGUE
TOUR TO BRITAIN

NORTHERN UNION 14 NEW ZEALAND "ALL GOLDS" 6 AT
HEADINGLEY, LEEDS, WEST YORKSHIRE LS6 3BU ENGLAND.
SATURDAY 25 JANUARY 1908.

The birth of rugby league in New Zealand came directly from the All Blacks' first rugby union tour of Britain (see 1905). During the tour New Zealander George W Smith was impressed by the Northern Union game (later known as rugby league), and accepted an invitation to return with a New Zealand side to play under NU rules. Smith and post office clerk Albert Henry Baskerville (aka Baskiville), organised a squad of paid players who were suspended by the New Zealand Rugby Football Union for professionalism and – despite playing in black – were dubbed the All Golds by the pro-Union press because they played for money. The All Golds landed at Folkestone on 30 September 1907 to play thirty-five games at a sport they had never before played. Despite the fact that only Smith knew anything about NU rugby, the tourists won their first game, against Bramley on 9 October, and went on to win nineteen, draw two and lose fourteen of their matches. England won the first ever rugby league Test match, at Headingley, but the All Golds won the series 2-1 after defeating England 18-6 at Stamford Bridge, Chelsea's home ground, and 8-5 at Cheltenham.

DID YOU KNOW?

One repercussion of the All Golds' tour that resonates to this day is that Wigan signed New Zealander Lance Todd immediately after the third Test. Todd went on to play for Dewsbury, manage Salford and commentate for the BBC, but his lasting legacy was giving his name to the coveted Challenge Cup man-of-the-match award. (See 1946.)

FIRST

FIRST
AUSTRALIAN RUGBY LEAGUE CLUB

FIRST
WINNERS OF THE
SYDNEY PREMIERSHIP

FIRST
CLUB TO RETAIN THE
SYDNEY PREMIERSHIP TITLE

NEWTOWN, FOUNDED WEDNESDAY 8 JANUARY 1908 AND SOUTH SYDNEY, AUSTRALIA. 1908.

After the All Golds had successfully introduced Northern Union rugby to Australia (see previous entry) eight clubs were formed to compete in the first Sydney Premiership. The first was Newtown, on 8 January 1908, and the remaining seven were: Balmain, Cumberland, Eastern Suburbs, Glebe, Newcastle, North Sydney and South Sydney. Souths emerged as the inaugural winners, beating Eastern Suburbs 14-12 in the Grand Final and retaining their title the following season with Balmain as runners-up.

To date, Souths remain the most successful Australian rugby league club, with twenty Premierships to their name (see also 1929). The Hollywood actor Russell Crowe currently owns a large stake in the club. (See 2006).

DID YOU KNOW?

The first two Grand Finalists, South Sydney Rabbitohs and Eastern Suburbs – now known as the Sydney Roosters – are the only two founder clubs still playing in the Sydney Premiership. (The current Newcastle Knights were formed seventy-nine years after the demise of the original Newcastle Rebels.)

ONLY
WELSH RUGBY UNION
INTERNATIONAL KILLED
BY A POISONED ARROW

NORMAN BIGGS AT SAKABA, KEBBI, NIGERIA. THURSDAY 27 FEBRUARY 1908.

Trinity Hall, Cambridge-educated Norman Witchell Biggs played club rugby for Cardiff and became the youngest player to represent Wales against New Zealand Natives on 22 December 1888 at St Helen's, when he was 18 years and 49 days old – it was a record that stood for more than a century before being broken by Tom Prydie in 2010.

In the opening match of the 1894 Home Nations Championship, Wales lost by 24-3 to England and Biggs was criticised for not tackling Harry Bradshaw, scorer of the first try. Biggs replied, "Tackle him? It was as much as I could do to get out of his way." Biggs also played cricket for Glamorgan.

After the outbreak of the Boer War, Biggs volunteered for service and was posted as a private to the Glamorgan Yeomanry and was wounded when he was shot through the thigh near Vrede on 11 October 1900. Four months later, on 16 February 1901, he was promoted to second lieutenant and became a full lieutenant on 17 April. Invalided home, he was commissioned as a lieutenant in the 3rd Battalion Welsh Regiment on 13 June 1903.

He was appointed an Instructor of Musketry on 10 May 1905. Seconded to the Colonial Office, he was sent to Northern Nigeria as a superintendent of police on 10 February 1906.

On patrol two years later, he was killed when a poison arrow struck him.

FIRST

NEW ZEALAND-AUSTRALIA
RUGBY LEAGUE TEST MATCH

FIRST

GAME OF RUGBY LEAGUE
IN AUSTRALIA

FIRST

GAME OF RUGBY LEAGUE
IN NEW ZEALAND

**NEW ZEALAND 11 AUSTRALIA 10 AT SYDNEY AGRICULTURAL
SHOWGROUND, MOORE PARK, SYDNEY, NEW SOUTH WALES,
AUSTRALIA. SATURDAY 9 MAY 1908 (FIRST TEST AND FIRST
MATCH IN AUSTRALIA) AND BLACKS 55 REDS 20 AT ATHLETIC
PARK, NEWTOWN, WELLINGTON, NEW ZEALAND (FIRST MATCH
IN NEW ZEALAND). JUNE 1908.**

While George Smith and Albert Baskerville were organising the All
Golds tour (see previous entry) the Australian Rugby Football Union
was going through similar "broken time" arguments to those encountered
in England (see 1895), and a group of rebel Australians invited the All
Golds to play in Australia en route to Britain. Because neither side
had ever played Northern Union rugby the three matches, all at the
Sydney Agricultural Showground, were played under Rugby Football
Union rules: New Zealand won all three, 12-8, 19-5 and 5-3 on 17,
21 and 24 August 1907. After their English tour the All Golds sailed
home via Australia where they played **the first Test series between the
two countries under Northern Union rules**, the first of which, on 9
May 1908, was the first game of rugby league on Australian soil. New
Zealand won the first two Tests eleven points to ten in Sydney and 24-
12 in Brisbane on 30 May, but lost the third 14-9 in Sydney on 6 June.
Baskerville died of pneumonia in Brisbane on 20 May, aged 25, so after
returning to New Zealand, but before disbanding, the All Gold squad
played a benefit match for his mother. Reds beat Blacks in the first NU
match on New Zealand soil, a high-scoring affair that attracted 6,000
spectators.

FIRST
ASHES TEST
FIRST
AUSTRALIAN RUGBY LEAGUE
TOUR OF BRITAIN
FIRST
ENGLISH TOUR
OF AUSTRALASIA

Northern Union (England) 22 (6t, 2g) Australia 22 (4t, 5g) at Park
Royal Ground (home of Queens Park Rangers), London NW10
England. 2.30pm Saturday 12 December 1908.

After just one season of domestic rugby league (see previous entry) the
Australians had mastered the game sufficiently to mount a forty-six-
match tour of Britain, arriving at Tilbury on 26 September 1908 and
leaving Liverpool on 11 March 1909. Their record was won eighteen,
drew six and lost twenty-two, including three Test matches, named the
Ashes series in emulation of cricket's iconic series. The first Ashes Test
ended 22-all in north London. Billy Batten (two), Ernie Brooks, Asa
Robinson, Johnny Thomas and George Tyson scored tries for Northern
Union while Brooks scored two goals. Jim Devereux (three) and Arthur
Butler scored tries and Herbert Messenger hit five goals. It was expected
that the match would raise "a substantial amount of money" but the
organisers were disappointed as fewer than two thousand spectators paid
to attend.

"This was to be regretted," *The Times* reported, as "the quality of
football seen deserved a much larger patronage". The tourists lost the
series 3-0, losing the next two Tests 15-5 at St James' Park in Newcastle
upon Tyne on 23 January 1909 and 6-5 at Villa Park in Birmingham on
10 February. England returned the compliment in 1910, launching the
first tour of Australasia in which they won thirteen, drew one and lost
four, winning both Tests against Australia (27-20 in Sydney on 18 June
and 22-17 in Brisbane on 2 July) and the only Test against New Zealand
(52-20 in Auckland on 30 July).

FIRST

RUGBY UNION MATCH AT TWICKENHAM

HARLEQUINS 14 RICHMOND 10 AT TWICKENHAM STADIUM, WHITTON ROAD, TWICKENHAM, MIDDLESEX TW2 7BA ENGLAND. SATURDAY 2 OCTOBER 1909.

England's Tests against New Zealand and South Africa had been sell-outs at Crystal Palace and the Rugby Football Union realised that being the only home nation without a permanent ground of their own they were losing revenue, so decided they needed their own purpose-built stadium. In 1906, the Rugby Football Union began their search and committee member William Williams (who played rugby for Harlequins and cricket for Middlesex) found ten and a quarter acres of market garden in Twickenham, Middlesex. It was bought the following year for £5,572 12s 6d and nicknamed "Billy Williams's Cabbage Patch". The first stands – east and west – were erected in 1908, holding 3,000 spectators each. The north was left open while terraces for 7,000 fans were situated at the south and behind that a vehicle park for two hundred cars/carriages was constructed. The total cost of £8,812 15s 0d was raised by debentures. To avoid flooding by the River Crane, the pitch was raised above ground level. Additional drainage was put in place and fences built at a further cost of £1,606 9s 4d. A further £20,000 was spent on roads and entrances for the first game, which was in the autumn of the following year when Harlequins beat Richmond. **The first international at Twickenham** was on 15 January 1910 when England beat Wales 11-6. During the First World War the ground was used to graze cattle, horses and sheep. In 1926, **the first Middlesex Sevens took place** at the ground (see 1926). In 1927 the **Varsity match was held at Twickenham for the first time**. Billy Williams died in his sleep at Hampton Wick on 14 April 1951. He was 91.

DID YOU KNOW?

When England met Scotland for the first international at Twickenham (on 18 March 1911) they could not find the ground's entrance and had to make their way in through the adjoining allotments.

ONLY
"FAMILY CHAMPIONSHIP
OF THE UK"

Williamses 8 Randalls 0 at Carmarthen, Wales. April 1909.

Billed as the Family Championship of the UK, this unique sevens match actually involved only two families, both from Wales – perhaps because no other family in the UK could raise the requisite numbers for a team. The seven brothers Randall, all steelworkers from Llanelli, played against the seven Williams brothers from Haverfordwest, who numbered three commission agents, one clerk – and three hairdressers. Despite their less physical jobs, and the loss of one brother early in the match, the Williamses won 8-0. Although it was a one-off family affair the £100 challenge attracted some thousand spectators, although they may have wondered what sport they were watching – Billy Bancroft, the referee, said afterwards of the scrappy encounter: "It was more like a wrestling match."

FIRST
RUGBY UNION
FIVE NATIONS MATCH

WALES 49 FRANCE 14 AT ST HELEN'S, BRYN ROAD, SWANSEA
SA2 0AR WALES. SATURDAY 1 JANUARY 1910.

For the first time the four-team Home Nations Championship became a quintet when France joined the competition. France had played their first international against the All Blacks on New Year's Day 1906 and then competed against the home nations of England (1906), Wales (1908) and Ireland (1909) before making the Four Nations the Five Nations the following year. The France team set off on 31 December 1909 but at the station found out that Hélier Tilh was unavailable due to performing military service in Bordeaux. The party including the fourteen players set off on the boat train from the Gare Saint-Lazare while the manager Charles Brennus stayed in Paris to look for someone to make up the numbers. Eventually Brennus chanced upon Joé Anduran who was working in an art gallery on La Rue La Boétie. It took some convincing on behalf of Brennus but finally Anduran collected his kit and set off for Wales. The home side took the French visitors to the cleaners and ran out f49-14 winners. Anduran did not merit a mention in any reports and never played for his country again. Four years later, he answered his country's call and joined the infantry. On 2 October 1914, the father of two was killed, aged 32, in fighting at Bois-Bernard near Lens.

DID YOU KNOW?

It was at St Helen's that on 31 August 1968 Gary Sobers became the first man to hit six sixes off an over in first class cricket. Sobers was captaining Nottinghamshire against Glamorgan and was about to declare, telling his batting partner John Parkin, "I think we'll have another 10 minutes." Then Malcolm Nash bowled the first ball of what was to become the most famous over in cricket. Sobers walloped it out of the ground. The second ball went the way of the first, hitting the upper storey of a house in Gorse Lane, alongside the ground. BBC Wales commentator Wilf Wooller said drily: "Glamorgan could do with a few fielders stuck on top of that wall over there." When the third ball went into the members' enclosure, Glamorgan captain Tony Lewis warned Nash to play it safe. But Nash dropped the next ball short and Sobers hooked it into the crowd behind him. One of the Glamorgan slips told Sobers, "I bet you can't hit the next one for six." Sobers replied, "Ah, that's a challenge," and duly hit the ball long and high. Roger Davis caught it but fell backwards over the boundary – the previous season Sobers would have been out, but a new rule introduced earlier in 1968 meant that it was yet another six. Almost as soon as the bat connected with the sixth ball, Wilf Wooller knew that history had been made — "And he's done it! He's done it!" he cried. "And my goodness, it's gone all the way down to Swansea." In fact the ball landed, appropriately enough, in the garden of The Cricketers pub, where it was found the following day by a schoolboy and later presented to Sobers.

FIRST

HOME NATION BEATEN BY FRANCE IN RUGBY UNION FIVE NATIONS MATCH

FRANCE 16 SCOTLAND 15 AT STADE OLYMPIQUE YVES-DU-MANOIR, COLOMBES, PARIS, FRANCE. SATURDAY 2 JANUARY 1911.

In the opening match of the 1911 Five Nations, Scotland travelled to the French capital fully expecting a victory over the hosts. The French played seven debutants while the Scots also had seven newcomers. The match was very tight and the 8,000-strong crowd saw the home side win by a point.

FIRST

FATHER AND SON TO REPRESENT IRELAND

FREDERICK SCHUTE: IRELAND 0G ENGLAND 2G AT LANSDOWNE ROAD, BALLSBRIDGE, DUBLIN 4 IRELAND. MONDAY 11 MARCH 1878; (FREDERICK) GEOFFREY SCHUTE: IRELAND 0 SOUTH AFRICA 38 AT LANSDOWNE ROAD, BALLSBRIDGE, DUBLIN 4 IRELAND. SATURDAY 30 NOVEMBER 1912.

There have been more than a dozen fathers and sons who have represented Ireland but the first were the Schutes. Father Schute (1852-94) played twice for Ireland while son Schute (d. 1970) played one more.

ONLY

INTERNATIONAL TO DIE
BEFORE HIS 20TH BIRTHDAY

RICHARD CALVERT STAFFORD. SUNDAY 1 DECEMBER 1912.

Dick Stafford was born at Bedford on 23 July 1893 and was selected to play for England against Wales at Twickenham on 20 January 1912. England won 8-0. The *Evening News* described him as "a veritable Hercules in strength and physique". He played four Tests and was assumed to have a long career ahead of him. In October 1912, he was out with a muscle strain but returned seemingly fit only to play two matches before taking to his bed where "the strain of his stomach [w]as apparently… aggravated by a chill on the liver". When he did not seem to recover, a specialist examined him and diagnosed cancer of the spine. Three weeks after the diagnosis, Dick Stafford died aged 19 years 131 days.

ONLY

TEST MATCH PLAYED
IN FOUR QUARTERS

NEW ZEALAND 30 AUSTRALIA 5 AT ATHLETIC
PARK, NEWTOWN, WELLINGTON, NEW ZEALAND
(RUGBY UNION). SATURDAY 6 SEPTEMBER 1913.

New Zealand is well known for its wet and windy weather, and in 1913 conditions at the Athletic Park were so bad that the referee, a warehouseman called Len Simpson – officiating at his first Test – decided that the rain and gale force winds were going to have an inordinate effect on play. His solution was to play the match in four quarters of twenty minutes each to share the wind advantage more evenly – the only time in either code that this has happened.

ONLY
10-MAN TEAM TO WIN
THE RUGBY LEAGUE ASHES

Rorke's Drift Test, Australia 6 England 14 at Sydney Cricket Ground,
Moore Park, Moore Park Road, Sydney, New South Wales 2021
Australia. 3pm Saturday 4 July 1914.

Even before the extraordinary events of the match itself began to unfold
this was set to be an epic encounter. Only eight days had been allocated
for the three-Test series. England won the first Test 23-5 on 27 June
at the Royal Agricultural Society Showground, Sydney before a crowd
of 40,000 and Australia won the second 12-7 two days later at Sydney
Cricket Ground before 55,000 spectators. The British tourists, with six
members of the first-choice Test team injured, complained at having to
play again only five days later but the date was set, and a telegram from
the Northern Union in England, misquoting Nelson, told tour manager
John Clifford: "England expects every man to do his duty". Before the
match Clifford told his beleaguered troops: "You are playing in a game of
football this afternoon, but more than that, you are playing for England
and more, even, you are playing for Right versus Wrong. You will win
because you have to win." Tour captain Harold Wagstaff remembered:
"The men in my team were moved. I was impressed and thrilled as never
before by a speech. You could see our fellows clenching their fists as Mr
Clifford spoke." And so the weakened side took to the field, establishing
an unlikely 9-3 lead by half-time. Then things began to fall apart: in a
ten minute period Douglas Clark smashed his collarbone, Frank Williams
injured his leg for the second time in the match and Billy Hall was
concussed. All three had to leave the field, leaving England (in the days
before replacements) with just ten men against thirteen – with half an
hour left to play. It seemed an impossible task but, rather then buckling,
England actually extended their lead to 14-3 before Hall returned for the
final ten minutes. Australia only managed to breach the English line once
more, leaving England with rugby league's most famous victory and a 2-1
series win. Even the partisan Australian pressmen were impressed: one
described it as "the greatest display of football courage ever seen", and
another likened the game to the infamous Zulu War Battle of Rorke's
Drift, as it has been known ever since. Those who played are honoured
with the letters "RD" by their names in the official rugby league records.

FIRST

WALES RUGBY UNION INTERNATIONAL
KILLED IN THE FIRST WORLD WAR

CHARLES TAYLOR: BATTLE OF DOGGER BANK, DOGGER BANK, NORTH SEA. SATURDAY 24 JANUARY 1915.

Charles Gerald Taylor LVO was born at Ruabon, Wales on 8 May 1863 and as well as playing international rugby for Wales was also that country's pole vault champion. Taylor made his debut for Wales against England in 1884 and played nine times for his country, the final encounter against Ireland in 1887 in a victory at Birkenhead. In June 1885, he became a committee member at the founding of London Welsh and played in their first game on 21 October. He had joined the Royal Navy on 1 July 1885 and rose through the ranks until on 7 February 1912 he was promoted to engineer captain. On 3 February 1911, HM King George V appointed Taylor a Member of the Fourth Class of the Royal Victorian Order. On 16 September 1914, in the second month of the First World War, he was posted to the battle cruiser HMS *Queen Mary*. On 20 November, he was transferred to HMS *Tiger*. Two months later, he was aboard *Tiger* when it fought in the Battle Of Dogger Bank. The German cruiser SMS *Blücher* struck *Tiger* and Taylor was one of the casualties. He was buried at Tavistock New Cemetery in Devon.

ONLY

RUGBY INTERNATIONAL
KILLED BY A RHINOCEROS

Denys Dobson. Ngama, Nyasaland. Monday 10 July 1916.

Denys Dobson was born at Douglas on the Isle of Man on 28 October 1880 and educated at Oxford University. He won three rugby Blues playing in the Varsity match in 1899, 1900 and 1901. He made his debut for England (the first of six matches) against Wales at Blackheath on 11 January 1902 and scored although ended up on the losing side. He also played four times for the British Isles. His sporting career over, Dobson was posted as a Colonial Officer to Nyasaland. In the summer of 1916, he was killed aged 35 by a charging rhinoceros. When news of his death reached England, a former Oxford lecturer noted that Dobson "...always had a weak hand off". (See 1904.)

━━•━━

ONLY
FIRST-CLASS RUGBY LEAGUE
PLAYER TO WIN THE
VICTORIA CROSS

LIEUTENANT JOHN 'JACK" HARRISON: OPPY WOOD, FRANCE. FIRST
WORLD WAR. THURSDAY 3 MAY 1917.

Schoolmaster Jack Harrison played five times for York RLFC during the 1911/12 season, while teaching in York, and made his debut for Hull FC on 5 September 1912 after returning to teach in his native city. He scored fifty-two tries in the 1913/14 season, which remains a club record. He was then selected for the 1914 tour Down Under but the tour was cancelled and instead Harrison found himself on a very different tour of duty with the East Yorkshire Regiment on the Western Front. On 25 March 1917, he won the Military Cross for leading a patrol into no-man's land and was gazetted on 17 April with the citation:

> For conspicuous gallantry and devotion to duty. He handled
> his platoon with great courage and skill, reached his objective
> under the most trying conditions and captured a prisoner.
> He set a splendid example throughout.

On 3 May, Harrison displayed even greater courage when the Hull brigade was detailed to attack the German lines at Oppy Wood, a well-defended area vital to the British advance. Harrison's platoon was pinned down by heavy machine gun fire and Harrison, armed only with a pistol and hand grenades, set about single-handedly eliminating the enemy position. His comrades looked on as he broke cover and weaved his way across no-man's land towards the German machine gunners before being shot down in the act of throwing a grenade into the machine gun post. The German gun fell silent, and 26-year-old Harrison was never seen again. On 14 June, *The London Gazette* carried the following citation:

> For the most conspicuous bravery and self-sacrifice in an attack. Owing to darkness and to smoke from the enemy barrage and from our own, and to the fact that our objective was in a dark wood, it was impossible to see when our barrage had lifted off the enemy front line. Nevertheless, 2nd Lieutenant John Harrison led his company against the enemy trench and under heavy rifle and machine gun fire, but was repulsed.
>
> Re-organising his command as best he could in no man's land, he again attacked in darkness, under terrific fire, but with no success. Then turning round, this gallant officer single-handed made a dash at the machine gun, hoping to knock out the gun and so save the lives of many of his company. His self-sacrifice and absolute disregard of danger was an inspiring example to all. He is reported missing; presumed dead.

King George V presented Harrison's widow, Lillian, with his Victoria Cross in March 1918 at Buckingham Palace. His son, John Jr, was killed during the Second World War in the defence of Dunkirk and is buried in that city's cemetery.

DID YOU KNOW?

In 2000, the Army rugby league presented the Jack Harrison VC Memorial Trophy to the Combined Services rugby league, to be contested annually in the Inter-Services fixture between the Army and the Royal Navy, and in 2003 a memorial plinth was erected at Hull FC's KC Stadium. Harrison's medals, donated by Lillian, can be seen at the East Yorkshire Regimental Museum, which is incorporated in the museum of The Prince of Wales's Own Regiment of Yorkshire in Temple Street, York.

LAST
RUGBY UNION INTERNATIONAL
TO WIN THE VICTORIA CROSS
ONLY
ENGLAND RUGBY UNION INTERNATIONAL
TO WIN THE VICTORIA CROSS
LIEUTENANT-COMMANDER ARTHUR LEYLAND HARRISON RN: ZEEBRUGGE RAID. FIRST WORLD WAR. MONDAY 22-TUESDAY 23 APRIL 1918

Four rugby union internationals have been awarded the VC (see 1899), the last of them – and the only English one – being Harrison, who was posthumously awarded the VC for his part in the Zeebrugge raid of 1918. Harrison was commanding the Naval Storming Parties aboard HMS *Vindictive* when he was struck on the head by a fragment of shell that broke his jaw and knocked him out. Regaining consciousness, he resumed command and led his party in the fatal but vital attack. His citation in the *London Gazette* ended: "Lieut-Commander Harrison, though already severely wounded and undoubtedly in great pain, displayed indomitable resolution and courage of the highest order in pressing his attack, knowing as he did that any delay in silencing the guns might jeopardise the main object of the expedition, i.e., the blocking of the Zeebrugge-Bruges Canal." Two hundred and forty British personnel were killed in the raid, and eight VCs awarded. Harrison's medal is on display at Britannia Royal Naval College in Dartmouth.

ONLY
INTERNATIONAL RUGBY LEAGUE
PLAYER TO GO OUT TO
PLAY BARE-CHESTED
PARC DES PRINCES, PARIS, FRANCE. THURSDAY 1 JANUARY 1920.

Prop forward Jock Wemyss made his debut for Scotland on 7 February 1914 in a 24-5 defeat at the National Stadium, Cardiff and three weeks later played in Dublin against Ireland when Scotland again lost. Then, like so many of his generation he found his career put on hold because of the Great War. Wemyss was recalled for his nation's first post-war match in Paris against France. He brought along his Edinburgh shorts and stockings and, having changed into them, sat in the dressing room waiting for his Scotland shirt. When the kit man walked straight past, Wemyss asked where his shirt was and was shocked to be told that he had been expected to bring the shirt he had been given in 1914. Wemyss explained that he had swapped it after the match against Ireland but the kit man refused to provide another shirt. It was not until Wemyss took his place bare-chested in the line-up that another shirt materialised.

DID YOU KNOW?

During the First World War Jock Wemyss lost an eye, a disability that he shared with his opposing number that day, Marcel-Frédéric Lubin-Lebrere (1891-1972). The two men became lifelong friends. It was said that Wemyss always carried a bloodshot glass eye and would pop it in when he was drunk so both "eyes" matched. He died at Edinburgh on 21 January 1974.

FIRST

REGULAR MEMORIAL MATCH
ESTABLISHED FOR A WAR HERO

FIRST

NORTHAMPTON PLAYER
TO CAPTAIN ENGLAND

MOBBS MEMORIAL MATCH IN MEMORY OF LIEUTENANT COLONEL EDGAR ROBERT MOBBS, DSO (1882-1917), NORTHAMPTON SAINTS AND ENGLAND AT FRANKLIN'S GARDENS, WEEDON ROAD, NORTHAMPTON, NORTHAMPTONSHIRE NN5 5BG ENGLAND. THURSDAY 10 FEBRUARY 1921.

Having celebrated his thirty-second birthday the day after Gavrilo Princip shot and killed Archduke Franz Ferdinand, the retired Northampton Saints and England three-quarter Edgar Mobbs was considered too old to be commissioned as an officer when the First World War broke out in August 1914. At the time he was manager of the Pytchley Auto Car Company at Market Harborough, having followed his father into the motor trade. Mobbs had also been thinking about emigrating to Canada. Not one to be deterred by the military knockback, he joined up as a private soldier and raised his own unit of 264 men as 'D' Company, 7th Battalion, Northamptonshire Regiment. Mobbs arrived in France in September 1915, and took part in the Battle of Loos. In March 1916 he was promoted to major and the following month took over command of the 7th Northants, later being promoted to lieutenant colonel. In August the same year, he was wounded during the Battle of the Somme by shrapnel in an attack on Guillemont. After two mentions in dispatches in 1916, Mobbs was awarded a DSO in December that year for his work as a battalion commander. In April 1917, the 7th Northants suffered heavy casualties during the Battle of Arras. Mobbs was wounded at Messines on 7 June but returned to the battalion on 26 June. A month later on 31 July 1917, the commander of the Mobbs Sportsmen's Battalion, aka Mobbs' Own, was killed aged 35 (The War Graves Memorial gives his age as 37) while attacking a German machine gun post that had trapped a detachment of his battalion at Zillebeke during the Third Battle of Ypres. His body has never been found and his name adorns the Menin Gate memorial. The battalion history reports, "The fact that his body could not be recovered and buried, as all ranks would have wished, was perhaps a good thing, as it helped keep alive his memory in the battalion, and inspired in everyone the resolve to avenge his death and to end the war that had already caused so much misery and suffering." It is believed that of the four hundred or so volunteers who served in Mobbs' Own, only eighty-five survived the conflict. In 1921, a memorial match was established, and every year until 2011 the Barbarians played an East Midlands XV at Franklin's Gardens, the home of Northampton Saints. In 2007, the match was transferred to Goldington Road, Bedford and in 2011 the Barbarians announced their withdrawal from the fixture. In 2012, it was agreed that the match would now be played against the Army alternating between Northampton and Bedford. Mobbs played 234 games for the Saints, scoring 179 tries, twice scoring six in a match. He also won seven England caps and in his last international, against France on 3 March 1910 at Parc des Princes, he became the first Northampton player to captain England. He is legendary for leading his men forward in battle by kicking a rugby ball ahead and following it up.

FIRST
RUGBY LEAGUE
FOUR-FIGURE TRANSFER FEE

Harold Buck, Hunslet to Leeds. England.
November 1921.

In November 1921, Leeds paid Hunslet £1,000 for the services of the winger Harold Buck. It was sixteen years after Alf Common became the world's first £1,000 footballer when he joined Middlesbrough from Sunderland on St Valentine's Day 1905. Common scored on his début in Middlesbrough's first away win in nearly two years and helped them to survive relegation. Buck's Leeds career was not quite as successful. He made his début on Saturday 5 November 1921 against Wigan but in his ninety-nine matches for Leeds was only the Headingley club's leading goalscorer once and never managed to break into the national side.

FIRST
USE OF TERM
BRITISH LIONS (RUGBY LEAGUE)
RUGBY LEAGUE TOURING SIDES, 1922.

According to the official British & Irish Lions website, the use of the term British Lions in rugby union dates from 1924: "The 1924 tourists to South Africa set out under the cumbersome title of the British Isles Rugby Union Team but returned as the Lions, having picked up their nickname from the heraldic beast picked out on their official ties." The tour was a disaster. Captained by Ronald Cove-Smith, the tourists were a weak side; mediocre players who would never normally have played were chosen. Of

DID YOU KNOW?

Alf Common was born at Millfield, Northumberland on 25 May 1880 and began his career with Hylton and Jarrow in north-east England before he signed for Sunderland in 1900. After eighteen appearances and six goals he joined Sheffield United in October 1901 for £325. He scored the first goal in the Blades' FA Cup Final win over Southampton in 1902. On 29 February 1904 he made his international debut against Wales – the first of three caps during which time he scored two goals in his second match (against Ireland on 12 March 1904. He played his last international game on 19 March 1906 against Wales). Three months later, his contract expired and he refused to sign a new one. In the summer of 1904, he returned to Sunderland for £520 and United's reserve goalkeeper Albert Lewis. In February 1905, he became the world's first £1,000 player when he joined Middlesbrough. They were in dire need of 5ft 8in Common's talents. The local paper reported, "He should prove a valuable acquisition to the Borough, who must win five out of their remaining 10 engagements to stand any chance of escaping relegation." Common's first game was ironically against his old club on 25 February 1905 at Bramall Lane. Boro won 1-0 and Common scored the only goal of the game (albeit from the penalty spot). It was Middlesbrough's first away win in nearly two years and they survived the drop. Common even took over as captain. However, the size of the transfer fee so amazed the footballing authorities that they set up an investigation to see if anything untoward or illegal had been carried out. As it turned out, Common's transfer was legitimate business but the investigators discovered that Middlesbrough had been paying illegal cup bonuses to players in the previous season. In five years at Middlesbrough, Common played 168 league games and scored fifty-eight goals. In 1910, he signed for Woolwich Arsenal and made his debut on 1 September against Manchester United. He scored twenty-three goals in eighty appearances while at Manor Ground, Plumstead Marshes, Kent before being sold to Preston North End in December 1912 for £250. Common retired from football in 1914 and managed the Alma Hotel in Cockerton and then a pub in Darlington up until three years before his death aged 65 on 3 April 1946.

the four Tests, the Lions lost three and drew one. Swansea wing Rowe Harding had an explanation: "Many unkind things were said about our wining and dining but that was not the explanation of our failures. The long train journeys (often of 48 hours' duration) and hard grounds took a heavy toll. The British pack was a very fine one; it was hardly ever worsted, but behind the scrums we hardly ever rose above mediocrity. The real reason for our failure was that we were not good enough to go abroad as the representatives of the playing strength of these islands." The British Lions term was first used officially for the 1930 tour to Australia and New Zealand. The use of the term in rugby league is less clear-cut because there is no record of when the name British Lions was officially adopted. Touring teams were known as the Northern Union XIII until 1922, when the NU changed its name to Northern Rugby Football League, and some league historians claim that this was the year in which touring sides began calling themselves British Lions. In his book *The Struggle For The Ashes II*, the rugby league historian Robert Gate notes: "From the earliest Northern Union tours until the last tour before the Second World War the Australian press invariably referred to British teams as England. For variety they tended to refer to the British as bulldogs or John Bulls. However, when it came to depicting them in cartoons or other artwork, it was almost invariably as lions mauling or being knocked about by kangaroos." So it seems that the concept of British Lions originated with the Australian rugby league press long before British touring sides – league or union – thought of using the name.

FIRST

TIME THREE PAIRS OF BROTHERS PLAYED IN A RUGBY UNION INTERNATIONAL

Hewitts, Stephensons, Collopys, Ireland 13 Wales 10 at Cardiff Arms Park, Westgate Street, Cardiff CF10 1JA Wales. Saturday 8 March 1924.

The 1924 Five Nations was won comprehensively by England, completing the Grand Slam, Triple Crown and winning the Calcutta Cup. By the time Wales met Ireland at the Arms Park in the eighth game of the season they had lost all their matches. Ireland created an unusual record by selecting three sets of brothers – Tom and Frank Hewitt were Belfast teenagers and both scored a try; George and Harry Stephenson also hailed from Belfast and Dick and Billy Collopy played for Bective Rangers in Dublin. Frank Hewitt was just 17 and the youngest player to represent Ireland – he played nine times for Ireland as fly-half between 1924 and 1927.

ONLY

RUGBY UNION INTERNATIONAL
TO WIN AN
OLYMPIC GOLD MEDAL

ERIC LIDDELL, FIRST TEST SCOTLAND 3 FRANCE 3 AT STADE OLYMPIQUE YVES-DU-MANOIR, COLOMBES, PARIS, FRANCE. MONDAY 2 JANUARY 1922. 400M AT PARIS OLYMPICS AT STADE OLYMPIQUE YVES-DU-MANOIR, COLOMBES, PARIS, FRANCE. FRIDAY 11 JULY 1924.

Eric Henry Liddell, nicknamed the "Flying Scotsman" after the record-breaking locomotive, was born on 16 January 1902 at Tientsin, north China, the son of a missionary. His story was partly told in the Oscar-winning film *Chariots Of Fire* (with some artistic licence). A fine athlete, Liddell played for Edinburgh University's 1st XV and won seven caps as a wing three-quarter, scoring four tries thanks to his remarkable speed. His first international match came against France at Stade Olympique Yves-du-Manoir, Colombes, Paris, (where he later ran in the Olympics), before a record crowd of 37,000. His last Test was the Calcutta Cup on 17 March 1923 at Inverleith, Edinburgh, before a crowd of 30,000, which included the Duke of York and was the only match he played in that Scotland lost (8-6). He then retired from rugby to concentrate on athletics and sixteen months later, he was representing Great Britain at the 1924 Paris Olympics.

By this time he was going bald despite being only 22 – his mother said the hair loss was the result of too many hot showers after training. The film is incorrect in stating that his family were opposed to him competing and also that the devoutly Christian Liddell only discovered as he boarded the boat for France that a heat for his best event, the 100m, was being held on a Sunday. He was aware more than six months before the Games began and began training for the 400m instead. Liddell still hesitated over whether he had made the right decision especially when he was criticised by some for being unpatriotic, Scottish nationals not having many chances for medals. On the morning of 11 July the masseur who had been looking after the British team handed Liddell a note. It read: "In the old book it says 'He that honours me I will honour'. Wishing you the best of success always." The quote paraphrased the Biblical quotation from 1 Samuel 2:30: "Those who honour me I will honour". Whether it was Liddell's supreme athleticism or divine inspiration is unknown, but he broke the existing Olympic and world records with a time of 47.6 seconds. Liddell celebrated his victory with a Tango Tea Dance on the Champs Elysées. After a triumphant return to Scotland, Liddell re-joined his father in China doing missionary work. He died of a brain tumour, weakened by malnourishment, in the Japanese Weihsien internment camp on 21 February 1945.

LAST
TIME RUGBY UNION
WAS PLAYED AT THE OLYMPIC GAMES
ONLY
NATION TO RETAIN AN
OLYMPIC RUGBY UNION TITLE
ONLY
RUGBY UNION PLAYER
TO WIN GOLD MEDALS FOR
TWO DIFFERENT COUNTRIES

DANIEL CARROLL, UNITED STATES OF AMERICA 17
FRANCE 3 AT STADE OLYMPIQUE YVES-DU-MANOIR,
COLOMBES, PARIS, FRANCE. SUNDAY 18 MAY 1924.

The USA may not have much of an international reputation for rugby union but they have been reigning Olympic champions since 1920.

Rugby union has been contested at four Games. The first was in 1900, when three nations competed: the French national team became the first champions after beating Germany (represented by Frankfurt) and Great Britain (represented by Moseley Wanderers who arrived on the morning of the match and left the same evening); no decider was played so Germany took silver and Britain bronze on points difference, both teams taking their medals without winning a game. The match between France and England attracted 6,000 spectators, and 4,389 of them paid for the privilege making it the largest attendance of any event at the 1900 Games. France's Constantin Henriquez de Zubiera (who also took part in the tug of war) was **the first black athlete at the Olympics**. Rugby was not played at the 1904 or the 1906 Intercalated Games. On the next two occasions only two nations took part: in 1908 Australia beat English county champions Cornwall, who were representing Great Britain, which meant that Britain took silver without winning a game. In 1920, the USA beat France 8-0 for the gold which, though the USA's first, was American captain/coach Daniel B. Carroll's second – he had won gold for the combined Australia/New Zealand rugby team in 1908 before emigrating to the States. The US team was also boosted by the presence of top sprinter Morris Kerksey, who won gold in the 4x100m relay and silver in the 100m.

Four years later the USA, featuring nine players from Stanford University, beat all-comers (i.e. Romania and France) to retain their title. When they beat the French national side 17-3 in the final (at odds of 20-1) the 50,000 partisan French spectators were so annoyed that they attacked the American supporters and one, Gideon William Nelson, an art student from De Kalb, Illinois, was knocked unconscious after being hit twice around the head with a walking stick. The team had to be escorted off the pitch by "dozens of gendarmes". France, having beaten Romania, took silver and Romania thus took bronze – the country's first Olympic medal in any sport – without winning a match. The team had some characters that achieved success in other fields. Linn Farish (1901-44) scored two tries in the final and during the war he rescued shot down airmen before he was killed in an aeroplane crash on 11 September 1944. He was posthumously awarded the Distinguished Service Cross although allegations were later made that he was a Soviet spy. William "Lefty" Rogers (1902-87) became a pioneer in chest surgery. Dud De Groot (1899-1970) coached the Washington Redskins; his winning percentage of .737 is the best in franchise history for coaches with at least one full season behind them. He later became one of America's leading oologists and ornithologists. Rudy Scholz (1896-1981) was still playing rugby at 83. Rugby sevens will make its debut at the 2016 Summer Olympics.

FIRST
RUGBY UNION PLAYER
SENT OFF IN AN INTERNATIONAL

CYRIL BROWNLIE, NEW ZEALAND 17 ENGLAND 11 AT TWICKENHAM STADIUM, WHITTON ROAD, TWICKENHAM, MIDDLESEX TW2 7BA ENGLAND. SATURDAY 3 JANUARY 1925.

Cyril Brownlie, a 6ft 3in loose forward, was the first man sent off in an international playing in the Test at Twickenham. The 1924/25 New Zealand team gained the nickname The Invincibles, after winning all thirty-two matches on tour.

FIRST
RUGBY UNION MATCH
AT MURRAYFIELD

SCOTLAND 14 (2G, 1DG, 2T) ENGLAND 11 (1G, 1PEN, 2T) AT MURRAYFIELD, EDINBURGH EH12 5PJ SCOTLAND. SATURDAY 21 MARCH 1925.

In the immediate aftermath of the First World War Scotland fared poorly against England until they moved in to Murrayfield and celebrated the official opening by registering their first victory in thirteen years, which also gave them the Calcutta Cup, the Grand Slam and all in front of a crowd numbering 70,000 (some sources say 80,000). It could have been so different – in the last few minutes England were leading eleven points to ten then Scotland scored a winning try.

FIRST
TEAM TO BEAT ENGLAND
AT TWICKENHAM

Scotland 17 (2g, 1dg, 1t) England 9 (3t) at Twickenham Stadium,
Whitton Road, Twickenham, Middlesex TW2 7BA England.
Saturday 20 March 1926.

From the hosting of its first international in 1910, England had been
unbeaten at Billy Williams's Cabbage Patch, the run extending to two
dozen matches. Then the Scots came to visit for the 1926 Five Nations
Championship. Scotland had begun their campaign on 2 January 1926
with a 20-6 win over France in Paris, while England kicked off a fortnight
later drawing 3-all with Wales at Cardiff. England lost to Ireland in
Dublin before convincingly beating the French 11-0 at Twickenham.
Scotland played two games in Edinburgh, narrowly beating France 8-5
and then losing 3-0 to Ireland. Fifty thousand fans including HM King
George V turned up to see if Scotland could retain the Calcutta Cup
and break the "Twickenham tradition". As it turned out they could and
did. *The Times* reported: "Slowness and hesitancy by ... the backs... and
some shockingly crude kicking ... robbed the attack of half its efficiency.
Scotland's chief glory... lay in the brilliant tackling."

FIRST
MIDDLESEX SEVENS COMPETITION

TWICKENHAM STADIUM, WHITTON ROAD, TWICKENHAM,
MIDDLESEX TW2 7BA ENGLAND. SATURDAY 24 APRIL 1926.

The Middlesex Sevens was initiated by Dr J.A. Russell-Cargill, a
London-based Scot, and played every May at Twickenham until 2001
when it was moved to August owing to a lack of available players in May.
The first winners were Harlequins and they held their title four years
running. The **last Middlesex Sevens tournament** was played in 2011
when Samurai beat Esher.

ONLY
NATIONAL NEWSPAPER TO FAIL TO
REPORT ON A TEST MATCH
BECAUSE ITS CORRESPONDENT WAS
AT A HOPSCOTCH MATCH

Samoa Times, *Western Samoa 5 Tonga 14, Apia Park, Western Samoa. August 1926.*

Until 1914, when New Zealanders supplied the Samoans with leather rugby balls, the islanders played rugby using coconut shells. Just ten years later they played their first rugby union Test match (losing 6-0 to Fiji) but evidently this remarkable leap from parochialism to the international stage did not excite much interest among the island press. On 6 August 1926 the *Samoa Times* reported: "[Our rugby correspondent] has failed us this week, and owing to a previous engagement at a hopscotch match near the Market Hall on the same afternoon we did not see the Rugby game."

LAST
RUGBY LEAGUE CLUB
TO WIN ALL FOUR CUPS

Swinton 11 Featherstone Rovers 0 at the Watersheddings, Oldham, Lancashire OL4 England. Saturday 5 May 1928.

From the institution of the County Cups in season 1905/06 until the abolition of the County League Championships in 1970, every club's dream was to sweep the board and win All Four Cups – Rugby League Championship, Challenge Cup, Yorkshire (or Lancashire) Cup and Yorkshire (or Lancashire) League Championship. In 1907/08, just two years after it became theoretically possible to do so, **Hunslet became the first club to achieve this remarkable feat**, largely due to their pack of forwards, who were known as the "Terrible Six". One of those six was J.W. Higson, who transferred to Huddersfield in 1910 – and then helped the Huddersfield "Team of All Talents" to achieve the same feat in 1914/15. The third and last club to win All Four Cups was Swinton, in 1927/28. On 19 November 1927, they beat Wigan 5-3 at Wigan before a crowd of 33,909 to win the Lancashire Cup, and on 14 April 1928 they beat Warrington by that same margin to win the Challenge Cup. On 21 April, the last day of the regular season, they topped the Lancashire League, which just left the championship play-offs. On 28 April, Swinton disposed of Hunslet 12-2 in the semi-final, and on 5 May they took the ultimate prize.

FIRST
RUGBY LEAGUE CHALLENGE
CUP FINAL AT WEMBLEY

FIRST
RUGBY LEAGUE PLAYER
TO SCORE AT WEMBLEY

FIRST
WEMBLEY RUGBY LEAGUE TRY-SCORER

WIGAN 13 DEWSBURY TOWN 2 AT WEMBLEY STADIUM, EMPIRE WAY, MIDDLESEX HA9 0WS ENGLAND. 3PM SATURDAY 4 MAY 1929.

The decision to take the jewel in rugby league's crown to the capital was an inspired one and, as well as bringing the game to a far wider audience, Wembley soon became an annual pilgrimage for many rugby league fans. The first final in the recently built Empire Stadium (then just six years old) brought mixed reactions from a national press more used to rugby union, one paper grumpily complaining, "It was rugger with the fun missing", while another commented, "Several of the players engaged in this game would be welcomed anywhere." On three minutes Wigan captain Jim Sullivan became the first rugby player to score at Wembley, with a penalty goal, and on fourteen minutes Wigan's Syd Abram became the first try-scorer. Just before half-time Dewsbury scored a goal to give themselves hope with a mere 5-2 deficit at the interval, but it was a false dawn – in the second half the Wigan half backs took control of the game and Wigan ran in two more tries to make it 13-2. Some 41,600 fans enjoyed a spectacle which prompted one journalist to contradict his fellow hack's comment about the fun being missing: "Most rugby union players will be grateful to the authorities for showing them the rugby league Cup Final, even though it made the average southern game look rather weak and watery."

FIRST
RUGBY LEAGUE CLUB
TO WIN THE SYDNEY PREMIERSHIP
FIVE TIMES IN SUCCESSION

SOUTH SYDNEY RABBITOHS. NEW SOUTH WALES RUGBY FOOTBALL LEAGUE, AUSTRALIA. 1929.

Having won the first two Sydney Premierships in 1908 and 1909 (see 1908), and two more in 1914 and 1918, Souths really stamped their dominance on the competition in the late 1920s. In 1925, the Rabbitohs went through the season undefeated, and won every Premiership for the rest of the decade to become the first club to win the title five times in succession; then, after relinquishing the title to Wests in 1930 they went on to win again in 1931 and 1932.

DID YOU KNOW?

There are several legends as to the origin of the Rabbitohs' nickname, two of which reflect the club's working-class roots. One is that in the 1900s, while still a rugby union club, players would earn extra cash on Saturday mornings by hawking rabbits with the traditional cry of "Rabbitoh!" often getting blood on their jerseys as they skinned the rabbits on the spot for their customers – opponents from the wealthier rugby clubs would see the bloodied jerseys and mockingly call out "Rabbitoh!" Another is that the name was a disparaging reference to the state of Souths' home pitch, which was said to be full of "rabbit 'oles".

LAST
OF RUGBY LEAGUE'S
"LOOSE" LOOSE FORWARD
RUGBY FOOTBALL LEAGUE, 1930

One of the more obvious differences between rugby league and rugby union is in the back row of the scrum.

When rugby league reduced the size of its teams to thirteen players it was two members of the back row who were dispensed with, leaving a back row of one – he was known as the loose forward because he was allowed to pack down on either side of the scrum. But in 1930 that changed with a ruling that the loose forward must pack behind and between the second row, "locking" the scrum as the lock forward does in rugby union.

ONLY
ENGLAND HOOKER TO
HITCH A RIDE TO AN
INTERNATIONAL IN A COAL LORRY
SAM TUCKER: ENGLAND 11 WALES 3 AT CARDIFF ARMS PARK, WESTGATE STREET, CARDIFF CF10 1JA WALES. 2.45PM SATURDAY 18 JANUARY 1930.

At 12:25pm on the day of the match, veteran England hooker Tucker (who had twenty-two caps but had been dropped for this game) was working at his desk in Bristol when the telephone rang.

It was Rugby Football Union secretary Sydney Cooper, telling him that England prop Henry Rew had injured himself the previous day in training and that Tucker, a First World War veteran who had been injured at the Battle of the Somme, was to get himself to Cardiff Arms Park as soon as possible. Realising that he had missed the train and with no Severn Bridge to ease his journey, Tucker called a taxi, went home for his kit, and then raced to Bristol's Filton Airport. At 1.50pm, he departed on a ten-minute flight in a flimsy biplane, which landed in a field on the outskirts of Cardiff. Tucker was badly shaken by the flight but grabbed his kit and ran across two fields to a road where he hitched a lift in a lorry to the Arms Park.

He then faced the problem of getting into the ground and luckily was seen by a local policeman who recognised him and eased his passage. Tucker arrived in the dressing room at 2.40pm, just five minutes before kick-off.

Dave Kendrew moved from hooker to prop to cover Rew, and Tucker slotted into his favoured position.

DID YOU KNOW?

Sam Tucker was determined to get to the match but his one regret was that the player who was on standby should he not arrive, Norman Matthews of Bath, not only did not get to play that day but was never selected for England again.

ONLY

JOINT TRY AWARDED IN INTERNATIONAL RUGBY UNION HISTORY

Wales 12 Ireland 7 at St Helen's Rugby and Cricket Ground, Brynmill, Swansea, SA2 0AR Wales. Saturday 8 March 1930.

When Ireland visited Wales in the 1930 Five Nations Championship, they had won two and lost one of their first three matches while the home side were looking for their first victory. In the first half Ireland were leading 4-3 when the Welsh forward Harry Peacock and wing Howie Jones dived at the same time to record the only joint try awarded in international rugby.

FIRST
TIME WALES BEAT ENGLAND
AT TWICKENHAM
ONLY
PERSON TO PLAY RUGBY UNION
FOR WALES AND CRICKET FOR ENGLAND

MAURICE TURNBULL: CARDIFF AND WALES (RUGBY UNION), GLAMORGAN CCC AND ENGLAND (CRICKET). ENGLAND 3 WALES 7 AT TWICKENHAM STADIUM, WHITTON ROAD, TWICKENHAM, MIDDLESEX TW2 7BA ENGLAND. SATURDAY 21 JANUARY 1933.

Turnbull began his first class cricket career with Glamorgan while still a schoolboy, and went on to captain Cambridge University (1929) and Glamorgan (1930-39). He played the first of nine cricket Tests for England in 1930, was named *Wisden* Cricketer of the Year in 1931, and served as an England selector in 1938 and 1939. An illustrious career (and all before the age of 33) but that was not all – he was also squash champion of South Wales and represented Wales at both hockey and rugby union, winning two rugby union caps in the 1932/33 season. His maiden rugby union cap came when he played scrum half against England on 21 January 1933, the day that Wales famously won their first victory at Twickenham – appropriately, the Prince of Wales was there to witness the occasion.

A major in the Welsh Guards, Turnbull was killed in action near Montchamp, Normandy, on 5 August 1944 at the age of 38. He was **the last Wales international to be killed in the Second World War**. His obituary in *Wisden Cricketers' Almanack* commented on his "sound and mature judgement" as a 17-year-old, which, wrote the obituarist, "encourages me to believe that, when a year or so later he sent for the majestic wine waiter of a London hotel and administered a rebuke on the quality of the claret, he was probably quite right!"

FIRST

RUGBY LEAGUE PLAYER
TO SCORE IN EVERY MATCH
OF THE SEASON
JIM (AKA JIMMY) HOEY: WIDNES, ENGLAND. EASTER MONDAY (17 APRIL) 1933.

Hoey, a goal-kicking centre who later converted to the second-row, had an uncanny ability to read the play which meant that he always seemed to be in just the right place to take the final pass of a move and score tries. He was also a master of the dummy, and one of the stories beloved by Widnes fans concerns the dying minutes of a game on 3 September 1930 at Headingley, in which Widnes were losing 9-7 to Leeds. Hoey took the ball near his own try line, sold one dummy on the halfway line, another on the Leeds 25 and a third just short of the Leeds line – the third one sent three would-be Leeds tacklers piling into a policeman standing on the touchline while Hoey skipped over the line for the winning try.

But his most famous record is scoring in every match of the season, a feat made doubly impressive by the fact that Widnes did not do particularly well in 1927/28, winning just half of their thirty-eight matches and finishing twelfth in the league.

Hoey was not the only kicker on the team but his name appeared on the scoresheet week in week out, league matches and cup-ties, so that when Widnes travelled to Barrow for the last match of the season everyone knew that a first was on the cards. Widnes and Barrow fans were there to witness it, but others had to await the match report, and as the score was read out it seemed that the unprecedented would remain so for a little longer – Widnes had lost 19-9, and they hadn't scored a single goal.

However, the result mattered little to Hoey, who had scored all three of Widnes's tries.

FIRST
LONDON RUGBY LEAGUE CLUB
ONLY
RUGBY LEAGUE CLUB
TO HAVE EIGHT INCARNATIONS
LONDON HIGHFIELD, WHITE CITY STADIUM, WOOD
LANE, LONDON W12 ENGLAND. 1933/34 SEASON.

Establishing a presence in the capital has long been an important goal
for the RFL. Early efforts included staging important Test matches at
the grounds of London football clubs such as Chelsea and Queens Park
Rangers, and, of course, playing the Challenge Cup Final at Wembley.
Then, in 1933, Londoners discovered they had their own club. European
sports fans may laugh at the idea that American moguls can uproot sports
teams like the Minneapolis Lakers (whose name derives from Minnesota's
state nickname "The Land of 1,000 Lakes") to Los Angeles (which has
very few lakes) but that is exactly what happened in rugby league nearly
thirty years before the Lakers' move. Wigan Highfield, who had finished
the 1932/33 season bottom of the league and with massive debts, were
saved from liquidation when the White City Company bought the club,
relocated it to White City Stadium and renamed it London Highfield.
George "Porky" Davies scored the new club's first try but the excitement
of this milestone didn't last and the White City Company pulled the plug
after just one season.

The following season, the club found a new home at Liverpool's Stanley
greyhound stadium and subsequently achieved some success as Liverpool
Stanley before moving to Knotty Ash in 1950 and playing as Liverpool
City. In 1969, the club was forced to move to Huyton, and played as
Huyton until 1985 when it moved to share a ground with Runcorn FC,
celebrating the past by playing as Runcorn Highfield. However, the past
was revisited in more ways than one, because in 1989/90 the club finished
bottom (see 1989), prompting another move and another change of name:
this time it shared a ground with St Helens Town FC and played simply as

Highfield. In 1995/96, Highfield beat all club records by gaining only one league point, in a 24-all draw against York, and the following season moved to Valerie Park, Prescot for its final incarnation, as the Prescot Panthers. After winning only four games in the next two seasons Geoff Fletcher, the chairman, accepted a one-off payment of about £30,000 for the Panthers to resign from the RFL. The club's last game on 20 July 1997 was a 72-10 defeat by Carlisle, who were also playing their final league game.

FIRST

RUGBY UNION PLAYER
TO SCORE FROM FULL BACK IN THE
INTERNATIONAL
CHAMPIONSHIP

VIVIAN JENKINS, BRIDGEND AND WALES: WALES 13 IRELAND 0 AT ST HELEN'S RUGBY AND CRICKET GROUND, BRYNMILL, SWANSEA SA2 0AR WALES. SATURDAY 10 MARCH 1934.

Jenkins made his international debut alongside his Glamorgan cricketing colleague Maurice Turnbull (see 1933) in Wales's first victory at Twickenham, and went on to become one of rugby union's finest full backs. Modern rugby fans of both codes are used to seeing full backs score tries but in the early days it was not only rare but actually frowned upon for a full back to attack: his job was to catch, tackle, and kick for touch. But Jenkins, who had played for Oxford University at centre and only switched to full back a few weeks before his international début, was used to attacking. In the last ten minutes of the game, with the scores at nil-nil, Jenkins fielded the ball in his own 25 and, instead of kicking, made thirty yards before passing to centre Idwal Rees who took the ball into the Irish 25 and passed to winger Arthur Bassett. Bassett was bundled into touch but not before passing inside to Jenkins, who had followed up and crossed for a try, which he then converted, inspiring Wales to score twice more before the final whistle. This audacious breach of convention (the coaching manual stated that he should have kicked for touch when he first fielded the ball) was not repeated in an international until 1962.

FIRST

RUGBY LEAGUE PLAYER
TO SCORE MORE THAN
400 POINTS IN A SEASON

JIM SULLIVAN, WIGAN, LANCASHIRE, ENGLAND.
SATURDAY 21 APRIL 1934.

Sullivan was, quite simply, a legend, and has been described as the greatest player of either code in any era. Born at Cardiff on 2 December 1903, he played rugby union for his native city at the age of 16 and within a year had become the youngest player to play for the Barbarians (at 17 years, 26 days) and had been given a trial for Wales. His reputation excited the interest of rugby league clubs including Wakefield Trinity, who sent him his rail fare to attend a trial, but Wigan got in there first by sending representatives to Wales, who signed him up for £750 on 18 June 1921 when he was still just 17.

It was an enormous fee at the time but has often been called the best bargain rugby league has ever known. He made his rugby league debut on 27 August 1921 against Widnes, scoring ten points in Wigan's 21-0 victory, and over the next quarter of a century he went on to play 928 first-class games, a record that stands to this day.

The hard-running, goal-kicking full back also still holds the record for number of appearances for a club (774), career goals (2,876) and goals in a match (22). He was **the first rugby league player to score at Wembley**, **the first captain to raise the Challenge Cup at Wembley** (after Wigan's 13-2 victory over Dewsbury, see 1929), and on 21 April 1934, in the Championship semi-final victory over Leeds, became the first player to score 400 points in a season; in Wigan's victory over Salford a week later in the final he brought his total to 406.

He would also have been the first player to go on four Lions tours Down Under if he hadn't refused the invitation to captain the 1936 tour due to his wife's ill health. His last game for Wigan was at Batley on 23 February 1946: Wigan lost 13-2 but Sullivan had the consolation of scoring Wigan's points. He stayed at Wigan as coach and then went on to become **the first person to coach St Helens to Challenge Cup success**, neatly reversing the result of his last game as a player, and repeating that of the historic first win at Wembley, with a 13-2 victory over Halifax.

He died at Cardiff on 1 November 1977.

FIRST

BRITISH CLUB SIDE

TO BEAT THE ALL BLACKS

ONLY

TIME THE ALL BLACKS

WERE BEATEN BY SCHOOLBOYS

WILLIE DAVIES AND HAYDN TANNER: SWANSEA 11 NEW ZEALAND 3 AT ST HELEN'S RUGBY AND CRICKET GROUND, BRYNMILL, SWANSEA SA2 0AR WALES. SATURDAY 28 SEPTEMBER 1935.

One newspaper critic, Old Stager, predicted that the All Blacks "may meet with an unpleasant surprise if they run against [Swansea] in foul weather", and he was proved right.

On a drizzly day, Swansea's half backs Davies and Tanner – cousins and both sixth formers at Gowerton County School – ran rings round the tourists, setting up an 11-3 half-time lead and, in the words of another Welsh critic, allowing rugby fans to "drink deeply of the champagne of the game".

Then the weather really closed in and the All Whites' pack managed to contain the All Blacks to a scoreless second half. All Blacks captain Jack Manchester said afterwards: "Haydn Tanner and Willie Davies gave a wonderful performance but please don't tell them back home in New Zealand that we were beaten by a pair of schoolboys."

FIRST

TELEVISED RUGBY MATCH (RUGBY UNION)

ENGLAND 16 SCOTLAND 21 AT TWICKENHAM STADIUM, WHITTON ROAD, TWICKENHAM, MIDDLESEX TW2 7BA ENGLAND. SATURDAY 19 MARCH 1938.

Television was starting to become popular in the 1930s. Highlights from Arsenal's 3-2 win in the opening game of the 1936/37 season were the first shown on television on BBC (the only channel at the time) on 29 August 1936. Only around 1,000 people saw the game on television. Just under two years later, rugby followed suit and the Calcutta Cup match between the auld enemies was the first to be televised. Scotland won the match, the cup and the Triple Crown.

ONLY

MAN TO PLAY CRICKET AND RUGBY TESTS FOR NEW ZEALAND

ONLY

MAN TO PLAY AND

OFFICIATE CRICKET AND RUGBY TESTS

Eric Tindill: Player: (Rugby) New Zealand 0 England 13 at Twickenham Stadium, Whitton Road, Twickenham, Middlesex TW2 7BA England. Saturday 4 January 1936. (Cricket) New Zealand 295 and 175 for 8 drew with England 424 and 226 for 4 declared at Lord's Cricket Ground, St John's Wood Road, St John's Wood, Middlesex NW8 8QN England. Saturday 26 June 1937; Official: (Rugby) All Blacks 9 British Lions 9 at Carisbrook Stadium, Murrayfield Street, South Dunedin, Dunedin 9012 New Zealand. Saturday 27 May 1950. (Cricket) England 374 beat New Zealand 142 and 133 by an innings and 99 runs at Lancaster Park, 30 Stevens Street, Phillipstown 8011 New Zealand. Monday 2 March 1959.

Eric William Thomas Tindill, OBE holds a number of records. He was the oldest Test cricketer at the time of his death in 2010, aged 99; he is the only man to have played Tests for New Zealand in both cricket and rugby union and the only man to officiate in both sports. An accountant by trade, Tindill also played football for Wellington in 1927, and was a founder of the Wellington Table Tennis Association in 1932. He played cricket for Wellington as a batsman/wicketkeeper from 1932/33 to 1949/50 and made a century on his first class debut on 20 January 1933, scoring 106 as an opening batsman against Auckland in a Plunket Shield match at Eden Park. He played five Tests for the Kiwis, four against England and one against Australia. His Test batting average was 9.12. With the oval ball, he switched between half-back and first five-eighth for Wellington (Athletic) from 1932 (his first match was against the All Blacks and the locals won 36-23) until 1945. He played in his only Test at Twickenham in the Obolensky match (see 1940). When he stopped playing Tindill turned to officiating. He refereed his first rugby Test at Dunedin between the British Lions and All Blacks in 1950. Nine years later, he stood in the cricket Test at Lancaster Park where England beat the Kiwis by an innings and 99 runs inside three days. He was inducted into New Zealand's Sports Hall of Fame in 1995.

FIRST
RUGBY UNION INTERNATIONAL
TO DIE IN THE SECOND WORLD WAR
FIRST
RUSSIAN TO PLAY FOR ENGLAND
FIRST
PRINCE TO PLAY FOR ENGLAND
FIRST
ENGLAND VICTORY OVER THE ALL BLACKS

H.H. Prince Alexander Sergeevich "Obo" Obolensky: Leicester Tigers and England. Friday 29 March 1940.

H.H. Prince Alexander Sergeevich Obolensky was the son of the Russian Prince Serge Obolensky, an officer in the Czar's Imperial Horse Guards who fled to London from Russia after the October 1917 revolution. The dashing, blond-haired winger, known to many rugby union fans simply as "The Prince", won two Blues at Oxford (and a fourth-class degree) before playing for Leicester Tigers (and later Rosslyn Park), and then causing a stir by playing for England while technically still a Russian – he was granted British citizenship later the same year.

When the Prince of Wales (later HM King Edward VIII) was introduced to the teams before Obolensky's international début on 4 January 1936, he reputedly asked the prince, "What are you doing playing for England?" Obolensky's response was to score two tries in England's 13-0 victory, their first win against the All Blacks. The first was a 40-yard dash down the right wing to open the England scoring, and the second is rated as one of the greatest tries in rugby union history. He took the ball on the right wing just inside the New Zealand half, and the All Blacks moved en masse to his side of the field to prevent a repeat of his earlier try. Reading the situation perfectly, Obolensky, instead of running down his touchline, crossed the field, and with the entire defence on the wrong foot managed to weave his way between them to score in the left-hand corner. He went on to win three more England caps that year (although he failed to score any tries), was selected as a member of the touring party for the 1936 British Lions tour to Argentina and appeared seven times for the Barbarians between 1937 and 1939, scoring three tries. Already an Acting Pilot Officer with 615 Squadron, Auxiliary Air Force at RAF Kenley, on the outbreak of the Second World War in September 1939, he joined the Royal Air Force's 504 Squadron. On 28 March 1940, he was recalled to the England squad to play Wales. The next day, he was killed during training, when he overshot the runway at Martlesham Heath, Suffolk, in his Hawker Hurricane Mark 1, plunging into a ravine and breaking his neck. He was 24.

DID YOU KNOW?

Obolensky was not the last RAF fighter pilot and Leicester Tigers winger with eastern roots to play for England – Rory Underwood made his début in 1984.

ONLY

RUGBY LEAGUE GOAL KICKED
FROM A DISTANCE OF MORE THAN 75 YARDS

ONLY

BRITISH FORWARD TO APPEAR
IN FIVE ASHES-WINNING SQUADS

MARTIN HODGSON: SWINTON 9 ROCHDALE HORNETS 5
AT ATHLETIC GROUNDS, MILNROW ROAD, ROCHDALE,
LANCASHIRE OL16 ENGLAND. SATURDAY 13 APRIL 1940.

Cumberland-born Hodgson signed for Swinton in January 1927 aged
just 17. By the age of 20 he had won all the major honours available to
him, having been capped for his county and his country, and having won
a Championship winner's medal, a Challenge Cup winner's medal, a
Lancashire Cup winner's medal and a Lancashire League medal (All Four
Cups – see 1928). He played his last game for Swinton in December 1940
but not before achieving a feat which has kept him in the record books
ever since – on 13 April 1940, in a match against Rochdale Hornets, he
scored what is still rugby league's longest recorded goal, a penalty kick
taken 77.75 yards from Rochdale's posts in a gale force wind. The rugby
league Hall of Fame describes him as "perhaps the most feared and
respected forward to play international rugby league in the 1920s and
1930s… Powerful, strong but agile and speedy for a second-row forward
of his time, he was punishing in defence and electric in attack".

FIRST

WALES INTERNATIONAL KILLED
IN SECOND WORLD WAR

CECIL DAVIES AT BAYEUX, FRANCE.
WEDNESDAY 24 DECEMBER 1941.

Cecil Rhys Davies was born at Pontypridd on 12 September 1909. On
20 January 1934, he made his only Test appearance in a nine-nil defeat
by England at Cardiff Arms Park. Two years earlier, he had become
the RAF heavyweight boxing champion. He was killed in action on
Christmas Eve 1941, aged 32.

ONLY
RUGBY LEAGUE CHAMPIONSHIP
DECLARED VOID
DEWSBURY STRIPPED OF THE CHAMPIONSHIP, ENGLAND. 1942/43 SEASON.

In 1942/43 Dewsbury came close to being the fourth club to win All Four Cups (see 1928) – and, were it not for their ultimate disgrace, they would in fact have swept the board because there were no county league championships between seasons 1941/42 and 1944/45. First, on 5 December 1942, was the Yorkshire Cup, in which they beat Huddersfield 7-2 on aggregate (several wartime cup finals were played over two legs, home and away).

Next was the Challenge Cup. In the first leg, on 24 April, Dewsbury beat Leeds 16-9 at home; in the second, two days later on 26 April, Leeds beat Dewsbury 6-0 for an aggregate score of 16-15 to Dewsbury. (Both sides fielded a number of guest players from other clubs, as was the norm during the war.) Then, on 8 May, Dewsbury's Treble dream fell apart when they lost 8-3 to Bradford Northern in the Championship semi-final, only to be restored when Bradford were disqualified for fielding an ineligible player. But if Dewsbury felt smug about their reprieve it didn't last long. They beat Halifax in both legs of the final to win 33-16 on aggregate, but were subsequently fined £100 and stripped of the title for the same offence as Bradford – fielding an ineligible player.

DID YOU KNOW?

Twenty-three years later, Dewsbury received another severe punishment after one of their forwards repeatedly roughed up John Warlow of St Helens in the 1966 Challenge Cup semi-final – an irate grandmother named Minnie Cotton ran onto the pitch and set about the offending Dewsbury forward with her umbrella: it turned out that Warlow was her lodger.

FIRST

RUGBY UNION V
RUGBY LEAGUE MATCH

**ARMY NORTHERN COMMAND RUGBY LEAGUE XV 18 ARMY
NORTHERN COMMAND RUGBY UNION XV 11 AT HEADINGLEY,
LEEDS, WEST YORKSHIRE LS6 3BU ENGLAND. SATURDAY 23
JANUARY 1943.**

For nearly half a century since the split between rugby league and rugby union, league players had been treated like pariahs and were barred from playing rugby union in case they tainted the rugby union players' amateur status – despite the fact that professionals at other sports were allowed to play rugby union. However, the war changed many things, and this was one of them – in January 1943 an Army rugby league XV beat an Army rugby union XV 18-11 under union rules at Headingley. The following year a Combined Services rugby league XV beat a Combined Services rugby union XV 15-10 at Odsal, Bradford, again under union rules, but there the thaw ended for another half a century – there wasn't another cross-code game until fifty-two years later, this time under league rules (see 1996).

FIRST

WINNER OF RUGBY LEAGUE'S
LANCE TODD TROPHY

**Billy Stott: Wakefield Trinity 13 Wigan 12 Wembley Stadium, Empire
Way, Middlesex HA9 0WS England. 3.30pm Saturday 4 May 1946.**

The Lance Todd Trophy, presented annually to the man-of-the-match in the Challenge Cup Final, is rugby league's most coveted individual award. It is presented in memory of the Kiwi who came to Britain on the first New Zealand tour (see 1908) and signed for Wigan immediately after the third Test.

Todd then made his name in Britain as a player for Wigan and Dewsbury and as the phenomenally successful coach of Salford – under his tenure Salford won three League Championships, five Lancashire League Championships, four Lancashire Cups and the Challenge Cup. The trophy that bears his name commemorates captain Todd's death in a car crash at Oldham on 14 November 1942, aged 68, and was first presented three and a half years later to Wakefield Trinity's captain and centre Billy Stott.

He missed three conversions but scored two tries and two penalty goals to register ten of Wakefield's thirteen points in their 1946 Challenge Cup final victory over Wigan – including the penalty kick, with 90 seconds remaining, that turned what would have been an agonising one-point defeat into a glorious one-point victory.

FIRST
REIGNING MONARCH TO
ATTEND A RUGBY LEAGUE MATCH
FIRST
PLAYER TO WIN THE
LANCE TODD TROPHY
WHILST ON THE LOSING TEAM

HM KING GEORGE VI: WIGAN 8 BRADFORD NORTHERN 3 AT WEMBLEY STADIUM, EMPIRE WAY, MIDDLESEX HA9 0WS ENGLAND. 3PM SATURDAY 1 MAY 1948.

Royal connections with rugby league began on 15 April 1911, when King George V became patron of the NRFU. He never attended a game and it was his son, the Prince of Wales (later Edward VIII), who became the first royal to attend a match when he attended a schoolboy match at Wigan on 23 November 1932.

Sixteen years later Edward's brother, by then King George VI, became the first reigning monarch to attend a rugby league match, as guest of honour at the 1948 Challenge Cup Final – a messy, scrappy affair of "missed opportunities and narrow escapes in defence". It wasn't a great royal display of rugby league but a reasonable amount of excitement was generated by the record crowd of 91,465 and the fact that only two points separated the finalists from just over a quarter of the way through until close to the end.

For the last ten minutes, the holders Bradford seemed poised to snatch victory, inspired by their indefatigable eighteen-stone prop Frank Whitcombe but in the final minute Wigan scored a second try to extend their lead to 8-3.

Whitcombe's consolation was that his "sure handling and shrewd kicking" had earned him the honour of being the first man to win the Lance Todd Trophy whilst on the losing side.

FIRST
OCCASION WALES WORE WHITE SHORTS
IN A RUGBY UNION INTERNATIONAL
Wales 9 England 3 at Cardiff Arms Park, Westgate Street, Cardiff CF10 1JA Wales. Saturday 15 January 1949.

Up until Wales's opening game of the 1949 Five Nations they had worn black shorts. Eric Evans, the secretary of the WRU, brought the new white shorts to training on 14 January.

The captain Haydn Tanner immediately expressed his disapproval, not because of the colour but the length – the shorts went down to the knees.

A team of seamstresses were called in and they worked into the early hours shortening the shorts.

It seemed to work because Wales won the match although it was their only victory of the tournament. The white shorts, however, were there to stay and only changed when BBC Television asked them to revert to black shorts so as not to confuse viewers watching their black and white television sets.

ONLY

ROMAN CATHOLIC PRIEST TO HAVE PLAYED INTERNATIONAL RUGBY

FATHER TOM GAVIN: IRELAND 9 FRANCE 16 AT LANSDOWNE
ROAD, BALLSBRIDGE, DUBLIN 4 REPUBLIC OF IRELAND.
SATURDAY 29 JANUARY 1949.

Despite being a deeply Catholic country, only one ordained priest has ever pulled on the green shirt in a Test match. Father Gavin was born the son of Irish immigrants at Coventry on 28 March 1922 and was ordained on 21 July 1946. He taught Classics for a year at Ampleforth, where he became a friend of Basil Hume, the future Cardinal Archbishop of Westminster. He made his debut at centre against France in 1949. John Henry McQuaid, Dublin's autocratic Archbishop, ordered Father Tom to stand down from the Irish team but the priest refused. It showed an independence of character that was to cost him promotions within the Church. He played in the next match a fortnight later – against England also at Lansdowne Road, which Ireland won 14-5. He was never picked again but maintained a love for the game. "Ireland changing rooms are pretty eclectic places and priests are very much part of everyday life in Ireland," Father Tom said a year before his death. "They certainly didn't tone the language down on my account. I love the modern game; it's exciting and very athletic. I'm all for it. Some of us oldies see our era through rose-tinted glasses. Rugby was always a fantastic game to play but I seriously wonder sometimes just how good a game it was to watch. Having said that, my fly half in my two Tests, Jack Kyle, was an absolute rugby genius, a star in any era. He was worth the admission price alone. Happy days. I would like to have gone on a couple more seasons." Father Tom died – also at Coventry – on Christmas Day 2009.

DID YOU KNOW?

Other priests have played Test matches but took Holy Orders after their international careers: Marnie Cunningham appeared for Ireland in 1955 and 1956 and Terry Curley represented Australia in 1957 and 1958. One other priest, New Zealander Paul Markham, later known as Father Paul Kane, played for the All Blacks against New South Wales in 1921, but that was not a Test match.

FIRST
CLUB TO APPEAR IN THREE CONSECUTIVE
RUGBY LEAGUE CHALLENGE CUP FINALS
ONLY
TIME THREE CONSECUTIVE
CHALLENGE CUP FINALS HAVE BEEN ATTENDED BY ROYALTY

BRADFORD NORTHERN 12 HALIFAX 0 AT WEMBLEY STADIUM, EMPIRE WAY, MIDDLESEX HA9 0WS ENGLAND. 3PM SATURDAY 7 MAY 1949.

In 1949, after defeat the previous year (see previous entry), Bradford Northern achieved a feat that would not be repeated for another forty-one years, until 1990 when Wigan won the third of their record eight successive Challenge Cup victories. However, as in 1948, the game was more memorable for the historic first than for the skills on display, and *The Manchester Guardian* summed up the disappointing game thus: "So Bradford won, but they did not enhance their own reputation nor that of the game."

Not only was it Bradford's third successive final, it was also the royal family's: in 1947 HRH the Duke of Gloucester watched Bradford beat Leeds 8-4; in 1948 HM George VI watched them lose 8-3 to Wigan, and in 1949 HRH the Duke of Edinburgh presented the cup to Bradford captain Ernest Ward after their 12-0 defeat of Halifax.

ONLY
COUNTRY TO FIELD
TWO RUGBY UNION TEAMS
IN FULL INTERNATIONALS ON THE SAME DAY

NEW ZEALAND 6 AUSTRALIA 11 AT ATHLETIC PARK, NEWTOWN, WELLINGTON, NEW ZEALAND AND NEW ZEALAND 3 SOUTH AFRICA 9 AT KINGSMEAD CRICKET GROUND, KINGSMEAD WAY, KINGSMEAD, DURBAN 4001 SOUTH AFRICA. SATURDAY 3 SEPTEMBER 1949.

The first Saturday in September 1949 was a dark day for the All Blacks. With their top thirty players on tour in South Africa, what was effectively a New Zealand third XV took on Australia in Wellington in the first of a two-match series. The Wallabies were winning 11-0 at half-time before 30,000 spectators and the brave All Black fightback wasn't enough to prevent an 11-6 victory for the visitors. Later the same day, in Durban, the All Blacks lost their third Test in a row to the Springboks. To make matters worse the tourists went on to lose the fourth Test in South Africa and the stay-at-homes lost the second against Australia – the only time the All Blacks have lost six Tests in a row.

FIRST
TELEVISED RUGBY LEAGUE MATCH
Great Britain 20 New Zealand 19 at Station Road, Swinton, Manchester, England. Saturday 10 November 1951.

Television began its relationship with sport in the 1930s, and the first televised rugby football match was rugby union's 1938 Calcutta Cup fixture (see 19 March 1938). By comparison rugby league came late to the screen, the first televised match being the second Test of the 1951 New Zealand tour, which Britain won by the narrow margin of one point, scoring four tries and four goals to New Zealand's five tries and two goals.

FIRST
TELEVISED RUGBY LEAGUE CHALLENGE CUP FINAL
WORKINGTON TOWN 18 FEATHERSTONE ROVERS 10 AT WEMBLEY STADIUM, EMPIRE WAY, MIDDLESEX HA9 0WS ENGLAND. 3PM. SATURDAY 19 APRIL 1952.

The first televised league match came two months later, on 12 January 1952, when Wigan beat Wakefield Trinity 29-13 at Central Park, Wigan. The first televised Challenge Cup Final came at the end of the same season – a superb final won by Workington Town under the captaincy of player-manager Gus Risman who, at 41 years and 29 days, remains the oldest player to have appeared in a Challenge Cup Final.

ONLY
AWARD-WINNING PLAYWRIGHT AND NOVELIST
TO HAVE SIGNED AS A SEMI-PROFESSIONAL
RUGBY LEAGUE PLAYER
TO PAY HIS ART SCHOOL FEES

ONLY
FILM ABOUT RUGBY LEAGUE
NOMINATED FOR AN OSCAR

DAVID STOREY, LEEDS, WEST YORKSHIRE, ENGLAND. 1950S.

David Storey was born at Wakefield on 13 July 1933 and is best known to rugby league fans as the screenwriter of the gritty 1963 feature film *This Sporting Life*, based on his own novel and starring Richard Harris as Frank Machin, a miner and Wakefield Trinity rugby league player who is trapped in a cycle of violence. (Harris was nominated for a Best Actor Oscar and his co-star Rachel Roberts was nominated for Best Actress – neither won.)

It was based at least in part on first-hand experience – Storey himself had played rugby league for Leeds, having signed up in order to pay his way through the Slade School of Art.

After leaving Slade he became an accomplished writer: his first novel, *This Sporting Life*, won the Macmillan Fiction Award, his second and third won *The Mail On Sunday*/John Llewellyn Rhys Prize, and a Somerset Maugham Award, and he later won the Geoffrey Faber Memorial Prize and the Booker Prize for Fiction.

He was an equally accomplished playwright, winning the *Evening Standard* Award for Most Promising Playwright in 1967 and the New York Critics' Best Play of the Year Award in 1969, 1970 and 1972 – the last New York Critics' award was for *The Changing Room*, another down-to-earth and gripping examination of life as a semi-professional rugby league player.

FIRST

BLACK PROFESSIONAL COACH IN
ANY BRITISH SPORT (RUGBY LEAGUE)

FIRST

BLACK PLAYER TO WIN A
GREAT BRITAIN RUGBY LEAGUE CAP

Roy Francis, Hull FC, England. August 1952/53.

Roy Francis had to leave his first club because the manager Harry Sunderland had no time for black players and was left out of the 1946 tour to Australia because of that country's colour bar. Francis made his only international appearance on 20 December 1947 at Odsal, Bradford, scoring two tries against the All Blacks in a match Great Britain won by 25-9. In July 1948, Francis joined Warrington for £800 and signed for Hull FC in November 1949 for a fee of £1,250. Francis played his last game on Boxing Day 1955 before switching to coaching. From the 1952/53 season Francis was made captain-player-coach: an historic appointment that saw him become the first black professional coach of any British sports team. Success was not long in coming – just three seasons later, in 1955/56, he led Hull to their first Championship title since the 1930s. The following season Francis's team lost by one point to Oldham in the Championship final, and the year after that, 1957/58, they were crowned champions for the second time in three years. (See also June 1954)

LAST

TIME RICHARD BURTON
PLAYED RUGBY UNION

RICHARD BURTON, UNNAMED TEAM VERSUS "A VILLAGE WHOSE NAME IS KNOWN ONLY TO ITS INHABITANTS". WALES. 1953.

Richard Burton once said that he wanted to be "the richest, the most famous and the best actor in the world". He achieved fame and fortune but squandered his chance of greatness because, as he told the *Daily Star* in a phrase which that newspaper later used as his epitaph: "I smoked too much, drank too much and made love too much." Born Richard Walter Jenkins on 10 November 1925 at the family home 2 Dan-y-bont, Pontrhydyfen in the Arfan Valley – the heartland of Welsh rugby – Richard was the twelfth of thirteen children of a miner, also Richard Walter Jenkins, and a barmaid, Edith Maud Thomas. His English teacher, Philip Henry Burton, MBE (1904-95), became his legal guardian on 17 December 1943 and nurtured Richard's acting talents and set him on the road to the West End and Hollywood – but not before Richard had been noted for his potential as a rugby union player. (Burton once said that the comment about his rugby-playing potential was the only review he ever kept.) In 1971, to mark its centenary, the Rugby Football Union published a collection of rugby writings entitled *Touchdown And Other Moves In The Game*, which included a piece by Burton entitled "A Welcome In The Valleys".

He revealed that he played rugby from the age of ten until the people employing him on stage and screen insisted that he should stop – if not for the sake of his "natural beauty" then for continuity purposes, because they couldn't shoot a mid shot of him on Friday with a straight nose and a close-up on Monday with a bent one, "so to this day there is a clause in my contracts that forbids me from... playing rugby football". His last game took place while he was playing Hamlet at the Old Vic (which makes it 1953 – indeed, he said later, "I would rather have played for Wales at Cardiff Arms Park than Hamlet at the Old Vic") against "a village whose name is known only to its inhabitants... with a team composed entirely of colliers... the kind of team where, towards the end of the match, you kept your bus ticking over near the touchline in case you won and had to run for your life." No one was supposed to know who Burton was, and he wore a scrum cap to try to disguise his identity, but as his team ran onto the pitch he heard someone shout "Le ma'r blydi film star ma?" ("Where's the bloody film star here?"). Dogged by thoughts of his career ending during that match, he nonetheless survived "with nothing broken except my spirit, the attitude of the opposition being unquestionably summed up in simple words like, 'Never mind the bloody ball, where's the bloody actor?' Words easily understood by all."

FIRST

DRAWN RUGBY LEAGUE
CHALLENGE CUP FINAL

FIRST

PLAYER TO WIN THE
LANCE TODD TROPHY TWICE

ONLY

BRITISH RUGBY FOOTBALL MATCH
TO ATTRACT MORE THAN 100,000 SPECTATORS

WARRINGTON 4 HALIFAX 4 AT
WEMBLEY STADIUM, EMPIRE
WAY, MIDDLESEX HA9 0WS
ENGLAND. SATURDAY 24 APRIL AND
WARRINGTON 8 HALIFAX 4 AT ODSAL
STADIUM, BRADFORD, YORKSHIRE
BD6 1BS ENGLAND. 7PM WEDNESDAY
5 MAY 1954.

The 1954 Challenge Cup Final at Wembley should have been one of the greatest ever – Halifax had finished the regular season five days earlier as league leaders, just one point ahead of Warrington, and both clubs had won their respective county championships. But, as so often happens in Wembley cup finals, caution stifled great play and the final ended with a try-less 4-all draw, two goals apiece.

The following weekend both teams were due to play their Championship semi-finals (both teams won) so the replay was set for the Wednesday after.

It became a legendary occasion in rugby league history. After such a poor final the pundits expected a mere 70,000 to turn up for the replay, but in the event 102,569 passed through the turnstiles – a record attendance for a British rugby match of either code even without the estimated 17,500 who got in unofficially, bringing the total estimated attendance to 120,000 (which would remain a rugby world record if proved: see 1999). The roads around Odsal were so congested that in order for the Halifax team to reach the ground the team coach had to be given a police escort down the wrong side of the road.

Many fans abandoned their cars and walked; others made do with listening to the commentary on their car radios, and some even prevailed upon local residents to let them into their houses to listen to the commentary.

Inside the stadium fans were climbing onto the roofs of the stands, and sitting ten deep on the speedway track that encircled the pitch. Sadly, for all the interest it was another dull performance, although the closeness of the scores kept things exciting: Warrington scored a try after nine minutes and, Halifax having had two "tries" disallowed, led 3-2 at half time.

The two teams then swapped penalties in the second half to bring the score to 5-4 before Warrington's Gerry Helme slid in for the winning try. Harry Bath missed the conversion, which meant that at 8-4 down Halifax were still within a converted try of victory. In the last minute Halifax's Stan Kielty launched a long high kick, which was caught by Arthur Daniels, who appeared to ground the ball for a try just before Warrington full back and captain Eric Frodsham turned him over.

However, referee Ron Gelder thought otherwise, and for a third time disallowed a Halifax try. The Challenge Cup went to Warrington and the Lance Todd Trophy to Gerry Helme, who became the first man to win it twice.

DID YOU KNOW?

On 8 May 1954, three days after the Challenge Cup Final replay, Warrington and Halifax met again in the Championship final at Maine Road, Manchester. Once again it was a close, low-scoring encounter, Warrington winning 8-7 to complete a memorable treble and leaving Halifax to rue the classic sporting disappointment: so near and yet so far.

FIRST

BLACK RUGBY LEAGUE
BRITISH LION

FIRST

RUGBY LEAGUE PLAYER
TO SCORE MORE THAN
35 TRIES ON A LIONS TOUR

FIRST

BRITISH PLAYER
TO SCORE FOUR TRIES IN ONE
GAME AGAINST NEW ZEALAND

BILLY BOSTON: WIGAN JUNE-AUGUST 1954.

The phenomenal Billy Boston, the son of a Sierra Leonean father and an Irish mother, never received an official honour but he was known as "The Wigan Peer". The rugby union skills he demonstrated with Neath and the Royal Corps of Signals attracted the attention of Workington Town and Hunslet but it was Wigan, after seeing him score six tries in the Army Cup Final against the Welsh Guards, that captured his signature, on Friday 13 March 1953 for a mere £3,000 (£75,000 at 2015 values). He scored on his Wigan first-team debut on 21 November, and after just six games of rugby league he was selected for the 1954 British Lions, becoming the first black player to tour Down Under, the youngest tourist to that date, the first player to score more than thirty-five tries in a single tour (he scored thirty-six) and the first British player to score four tries in a Test against New Zealand.

The Welsh try-scoring machine went on to twice score seven tries in a match for Wigan, and ended his career with 571 tries in 565 games before retiring to become landlord of The Griffin, a stone's throw from Wigan's Central Park ground.

DID YOU KNOW?

In addition to all his firsts, Billy Boston also remains the fastest "Try Centurion" in rugby league. When Martin Offiah scored his hundredth try in 1989, after just seventeen and a half months in rugby league, it was hailed as the fastest hundred tries in the sport. But a look at the record books shows that while Offiah's was the fastest in calendar terms he took eighty games to score them – whereas Boston's first hundred, though they took twenty-one months, came in a mere sixty-eight games. He scored his hundredth on Monday 12 September 1955 for Other Nationalities in the twenty-seventh minute of their 33-16 victory over England at Wigan's Central Park. (See also 1952)

FIRST

RUGBY WORLD CUP (RUGBY LEAGUE)

GREAT BRITAIN 16 FRANCE 12 AT PARC DES PRINCES, PARIS, FRANCE. 3PM SATURDAY 13 NOVEMBER 1954.

The driving force behind the rugby league World Cup – the first such competition in either code – came from France via its young rugby league president Paul Barrière (1920-2008), who donated the World Cup trophy.

The French proposed the idea as early as 1935, and when the idea was raised again in 1952 it was the French who agreed to host the first competition, which took place in October and November 1954. The Australians were not keen but when the French rugby authorities agreed to cover their expenses they acquiesced to taking part. (The football World Cup had a similar problem in its primary tournament.

Most European countries were reluctant to undertake the arduous journey to South America for the first tournament in Uruguay in 1930. The Uruguayan Football Association wrote to the Football Association extending an invitation to England, Ireland, Scotland and Wales even though they were not members of FIFA at the time, having resigned in 1928 in a disagreement over payments to amateurs. The FA declined on 18 November 1929.

Eventually after some cajoling four European teams – Belgium, France, Romania, and Yugoslavia – boarded ships to Uruguay.) Only four teams entered the competition. **The first World Cup tie took place on 30 October in Paris**: France beat New Zealand 22-13 at the Parc des Princes.

Great Britain were dismissed as no-hopers because all but three players had withdrawn from the team having just returned from an Australian tour, but managed to top the table on points' difference after Australia, France, Great Britain and New Zealand had all played each other. Great Britain and France had each won two of their three games and drawn with each other 13-all in Toulouse, setting things up for an exciting finale.

The play-off took place in Paris on 13 November, Great Britain running out 16-12 winners to claim the world's first rugby league World Cup. Scotsman Dave Valentine was **the first captain to lift the World Cup**.

DID YOU KNOW?

Only three teams have won the World Cup in the fourteen tournaments to have been held since 1954 – Great Britain have won it three times, Australia ten times.

The last time GB won was on 11 November 1972 at the Stade de Gerland in Lyon, France; they will never win again because, since 1995, the home nations have competed separately. The cost of the Millennium World Cup was so great that there was no competition for eight years, when the All Blacks triumphed in 2008 (beating host nation Australia).

FIRST
BRITISH JOURNALISTS TO REPORT
A RUGBY UNION LIONS TOUR
Viv Jenkins and Bryn Thomas: British Lions to South Africa.
Wednesday 22 June-Wednesday 28 September 1955.

The first Test of the 1955 Lions tour of South Africa, on 6 August, was hailed as the greatest Test of all time. Some 95,000 people packed into Ellis Park to watch South Africa go 11-8 ahead by half-time. In a pulsating second half the Lions scored fifteen points without reply to lead 23-11, then South Africa clawed their way back into the game, scoring a try in the third minute of injury time that took the scores to 23-22 with a conversion still to come. The unerring Jack van der Schyff, known as "the automaton", lined up his kick… and missed, giving the Lions a memorable one-point victory. For the first time the tour was reported by British journalists: ex-Wales international Viv Jenkins for *The Sunday Times* and Bryn Thomas for *The Western Mail*, who wrote of the first Test: "From the first whistle to the last the match produced an atmosphere of intense excitement with swift moving play of exceptionally high standard. Such a match comes but once in a generation."

ONLY
WINNERS OF RUGBY LEAGUE
ITV FLOODLIT COMPETITION
WARRINGTON 43 LEIGH 18 AT LOFTUS ROAD STADIUM, SOUTH
AFRICA ROAD, SHEPHERD'S BUSH, LONDON W12 7PJ ENGLAND.
WEDNESDAY 16 NOVEMBER 1955.

ITV launched on 22 September 1955 and in October and November of that year, the company sponsored the Independent Television Trophy, which saw eight clubs competing in floodlit games staged at London football grounds, with coverage broadcast locally in the south of England. The competition did not prove a great success and was abandoned after a single season, Warrington becoming the first, last and only winners in a nine-try cup final demolition of Leigh.

LAST
TIME AN ENTIRE SIDE
LEFT THE FIELD DURING A
RUGBY UNION INTERNATIONAL

**Wales 6 Ireland 5 at Cardiff Arms Park, Westgate Street, Cardiff
CF10 1JA Wales. Saturday 9 March 1957.**

The 1957 Wales v Ireland fixture took place in an absolute downpour,
and within minutes the pitch had been churned up into a quagmire. After
an hour, with Ireland leading, the teams were so muddy that referee Jack
Taylor could not tell them apart, and asked both sides whether they
wanted to change into clean kit. Wales accepted, and the entire side left
the field while the Irish ran on the spot, trying to keep warm while the
Welsh changed into dry jerseys – on their return the Welsh managed to
force a penalty converted by Terry Davies, which won them the game.
The International Board was not impressed with Scotsman Taylor's
decision – he did not referee an international for another three years, and
the rules were changed for the 1957/58 season to prohibit either team
leaving the field between kick-off and full time.

ONLY
TIME WALES PLAYED A
RUGBY UNION TEST MATCH
WITH TRIAL JERSEYS

WALES 3 ENGLAND 3 AT TWICKENHAM STADIUM, WHITTON
ROAD, TWICKENHAM, MIDDLESEX TW2 7BA ENGLAND.
SATURDAY 18 JANUARY 1958.

When the Welsh team arrived at Billy Williams's Cabbage Patch for their
opening match of the Five Nations competition, the kit manager handed
out the red shirts provided by the manufacturer. No one spotted the error
then or during the game that they were trial jerseys and not the proper
badged ones. "It was amazing that no one noticed," said Bill Clement,
the secretary of the Welsh Rugby Union.

ONLY

RUGBY LEAGUE PLAYER
TO PLAY A TEST MATCH
WITH A BROKEN ARM

**ALAN PRESCOTT: BRITISH LIONS 25 AUSTRALIA 18 AT
THE BRISBANE EXHIBITION GROUND, 600 GREGORY
TERRACE, BOWEN HILLS, BRISBANE, QUEENSLAND 4006
AUSTRALIA. SATURDAY 5 JULY 1958.**

The 1958 British Lions, captained by Alan Prescott of St Helens,
unexpectedly lost the first Test in Sydney by 25-8, so it was vital they win
the second Test to be played at Brisbane to keep the series alive. Things
began badly when Prescott broke his right forearm in the third minute
of the match but he simply had it strapped up and played on, determined
not to let the Australians know how badly injured he was.

During the next seventeen minutes centre Jim Challinor (shoulder)
full back Eric Fraser (elbow) and loose forward Vince Karalius (back)
were all injured so badly they were hospitalised after the match, and
stand off David Bolton broke his collarbone and had to leave the field.
Despite this Great Britain managed to forge a half time lead of 10-2.

During the break an Australian doctor told Prescott that his arm was
broken so badly that it was too dangerous for him to return to the field,
to which Prescott famously replied: "I'll play on, say nowt to nobody."
He returned and inspired his team to extend their lead to thirteen points,
but then the margin began to narrow: 20-10, 20-13, 25-13, 25-18.
But Prescott, arm hanging by his side, stirred his men to hang on for a
memorable victory to level the series.

Afterwards team manager Tom Mitchell wrote in his match report to
rugby league headquarters:

> This match had everything. High drama, pathos, fortitude
> and endurance stretched to breaking point, sheer naked
> guts and courage. Occasional flashes of humour on the field
> served but to highlight the grimness and intensity of an epic

struggle for mastery, for make no mistake about it, Australia brought everything out of their repertoire in an attempt to defeat us, feeling that they MUST on grounds of prestige alone win the day against a sadly depleted foe… The scene in the English dressing room at half-time will live long in my memory.

Very few (if any) of the players knew the extent of Prescott's injury, but it could not be kept from them. When they realised, in addition to Bolton's collarbone, the captain had a broken arm, they looked stunned. I daresay one or two could see a second-half victory would be snatched from them…

In the final analysis, his presence on the field meant everything… As you can well realise, this was a game of emotion, and as I write many hours later, I feel drained from the drama and tragedy of the game.

I feel sure this match will go down in the history of Australian and English [sic] rugby league Football as a great classic, and no better name can describe it than Prescott's Epic.

FIRST

PLAYER TO PLAY FOR BRITISH LIONS AND AGAINST THEM

TOM REID: EASTERN CANADA 6 BRITISH LIONS 70 AT VARSITY STADIUM, TORONTO, ONTARIO, CANADA. THURSDAY 29 SEPTEMBER 1959.

Tom Reid played for the British Lions on their 1955 tour to South Africa, playing in two of the four Tests (see 1955), and four years later became the first player to play against the Lions when he represented Eastern Canada.

LAST

TIME FIVE BROTHERS PLAYED ON THE SAME FIRST-CLASS RUGBY UNION TEAM

CLARKE BROTHERS: WAIKATO 11 THAMES VALLEY 8 AT SPORTS DOMAIN, TE AROHA, WAIKATO, NORTH ISLAND, NEW ZEALAND. SATURDAY 12 AUGUST 1961.

Remarkably, five brothers have played in first class teams on two occasions, both in New Zealand. The first were the Smith brothers – full back George, centre Bill and forwards Gordon, Bob and Campbell – who played together for Bush in Bush's 16-0 defeat by Wairarapa in Greytown, New Zealand, in July 1903. The second and last were the Clarkes – full back Don, centre Doug, prop Ian and second rowers Graeme and Brian – who played in Waikato province's victory over Thames Valley at Te Aroha in the summer of 1961.

FIRST

RUGBY UNION INTERNATIONAL CHAMPIONSHIP TO END THE SEASON AFTER IT STARTED

Ireland 3 Wales 3 at Lansdowne Road, Ballsbridge, Dublin 4 Republic of Ireland. Saturday 17 November 1962.

A smallpox outbreak in South Wales led to the postponement of several sporting fixtures at the start of 1962 for fear of spreading the disease. Among the postponed matches was Wales's scheduled visit to Ireland on 10 March, which was rearranged for 28 April, the last weekend of the season. Unfortunately a fresh outbreak of smallpox meant that this, too, had to be postponed and the fixture was finally played the following season, on 17 November: the 3-all draw left Ireland with the Wooden Spoon.

FIRST

RUGBY LEAGUE CLUB
TO INSTALL UNDER SOIL HEATING
LEEDS AT HEADINGLEY, LEEDS, WEST YORKSHIRE LS6 3BU ENGLAND. APRIL 1963.

During the winter of 1962/63 bad weather and frozen pitches led to so many postponed matches that the season was extended until 1 June. Champions Swinton played no less than fourteen matches in April and May, and in one gruelling week played Oldham on 12 April, St Helens at home on 13 April and St Helens away on 15 April – and won all three. That same April, Leeds ensured that they would rarely ever again have to postpone a match, by installing under soil heating at Headingley at a cost of £6,488 – the system comprised thirty-eight miles of electric wiring buried six inches beneath the surface of the pitch.

ONLY

OCCASION NATIONAL ANTHEM
NOT PLAYED AT A
TWICKENHAM TEST
England 0 New Zealand 14 at Twickenham Stadium, Whitton Road, Twickenham, Middlesex TW2 7BA England. Saturday 4 January 1964

The teams came out on to the pitch as normal to warm up but then were told to return to their dressing rooms. The band also left the pitch and did not return to play the National Anthem, the only time in modern history that *God Save The Queen* has not resonated around Twickenham in a Test match.

FIRST
PAIR OF RUGBY LEAGUE PLAYERS
TO SHARE THE LANCE TODD TROPHY

RAY ASHBY AND BRIAN GABBITAS: WIGAN 20 HUNSLET
16 AT WEMBLEY STADIUM, EMPIRE WAY, MIDDLESEX
HA9 0WS ENGLAND. 3PM SATURDAY 8 MAY 1965.

The result of this mismatch between the mighty Wigan and the relatively humble Parksiders was much closer than anyone expected. One newspaper reported: "Eighty minutes of fast, open football with only four points between the sides at the end of them. Such was the outcome of the best rugby league Challenge Cup Final seen at Wembley for many years", and it is still remembered as one of the best ever. It is also remarkable as the first occasion on which the Lance Todd Trophy was shared – something that would not be repeated until 2007, in the first final at the newly re-opened Wembley Stadium. (See 2007)

ONLY
WINNERS OF RUGBY LEAGUE
BOTTOM FOURTEEN COMPETITION

ONLY
CUP FINAL APPEARANCE
BY DONCASTER

HUDDERSFIELD 13 DONCASTER 3 AT TATTERSFIELD,
BENTLEY ROAD, DONCASTER, YORKSHIRE, DN5
ENGLAND. TUESDAY 18 MAY 1965.

It was an idea that was never destined for success. When rugby league reverted to a one-division format in the season 1964/65 the top sixteen clubs played off for the Championship title and the bottom fourteen were invited to compete in a competition named by someone who had clearly never attended a marketing and PR course, or had any sense of tact – the splendidly named Bottom Fourteen Competition. Only ten of the bottom fourteen accepted their invitations to compete, and the fans were equally uninspired, the tournament attracting an average gate of less than 2,000 – although on the positive side it did allow Doncaster to make the only cup final appearance in the club's history. This ludicrous idea was scrapped after one season, Huddersfield being the only club ever crowned kings of the Bottom Fourteen.

———•◦×◦•———

FIRST
WINNERS OF RUGBY LEAGUE BBC2 FLOODLIT TROPHY

ONLY
CLUB TO WIN BBC2 FLOODLIT TROPHY
THREE TIMES IN SUCCESSION

CASTLEFORD (FIRST WINNERS) TUESDAY 14 DECEMBER 1965, CASTLEFORD (THREE-TIME WINNERS) TUESDAY 16 JANUARY 1968.

In the mid-Sixties Castleford's open style of play earned them the nickname Classy Cas, and it was a style they seemed to be able to turn on for cup competitions in front of the television cameras, winning the BBC2 Floodlit Trophy in 1965, 1966 and 1967, and the Challenge Cup in 1969 and 1970. The year 1965 was a landmark for Castleford when they were among the first clubs to install permanent floodlights. The new lights were inaugurated on 20 September when Yorkshire beat New Zealand 15-9 at Castleford's Wheldon Road ground, and just five weeks later, on 26 October, Castleford drew with Leeds in the opening round of the first BBC2 Floodlit Trophy.

The competition was open to all clubs with permanent floodlights, which was just eight clubs in 1965, rising to twenty-two by the final competition in 1979. Matches were played on Tuesday nights, the second half being screened live from 8.10pm, and the final was usually played at one of the finalists' grounds, decided by a draw. For the first three years, Castleford made the trophy their own, beating St Helens 4-0 at St Helens in the first final, Swinton 7-2 at Castleford in the second and Leigh 8-5 at Leeds in the third.

DID YOU KNOW?

The only BBC2 Floodlit Trophy Final played in daylight was the 1973 final on Tuesday 18 December in which Bramley beat Widnes by 15-7 – the ultimate match kicked off early enough to be played in daylight because of a national power strike. It was Bramley's first cup success since the club had been founded in 1879, ninety-four years earlier, and remains their only cup success to date.

ONLY

RUGBY LEAGUE CLUB
TO WIN ELEVEN
SYDNEY PREMIERSHIPS IN A ROW

ST GEORGE 23 BALMAIN 4 AT SYDNEY CRICKET GROUND, MOORE PARK, MOORE PARK ROAD, SYDNEY, NEW SOUTH WALES 2021 AUSTRALIA. SUNDAY 18 SEPTEMBER 1966.

For twenty-three seasons in a row, from 1949 until 1971 inclusive, either South Sydney or St George – or, on four occasions, both – appeared in the Sydney Grand Final. For twenty-one of those twenty-three seasons – including sixteen in a row from 1953 until 1968 – either South Sydney or St George took the title. This remarkable duopoly began in 1949 when St George beat South Sydney 19-12. South Sydney won five of the next six titles and then, in 1956, St George began their unparalleled run of eleven wins during which they beat South Sydney and Eastern Suburbs once each, Manly twice, Balmain three times and Western Suburbs four times. Then South Sydney took over the reins again, winning four of the next five Grand Finals. The duoploy ended in 1971 in a neat reversal of the way it had begun, with South Sydney beating St George 16-10. Then some of the other clubs got a look-in. (See 1956)

ONLY

BRITISH PRIME MINISTER TO LOSE AN EYE PLAYING RUGBY

Rt. Hon. Gordon Brown: Kirkcaldy High School, Dunnikier Way,
Kirkcaldy, Fife KY1 3LR Scotland. April 1967

Gordon Brown attended Kirkcaldy High School and two years earlier than normal he won a place at the University of Edinburgh to study history. A keen sportsman, he took part in an end of term rugby match and was kicked in the head causing the retina in his left eye to become detached, eventually leaving him blind. He underwent several operations and spent six months laying still with his eyes covered in a dark room but his sight could not be saved. Brown later recalled: "It was the first two minutes of the game and I was caught in a loose scrum when someone kicked me in the head. We were a school team playing former pupils, and everyone was trying to assert how strong and powerful they were. They probably decided to go for it in the first few minutes and give these young guys a shock. I got kicked unconscious, came around and just kept playing, because I didn't know anything was wrong at the time."

LAST

REIGNING BRITISH MONARCH TO ATTEND A RUGBY LEAGUE CHALLENGE CUP FINAL

ONLY

REFEREE TO OFFICIATE AT TWO ROYAL CHALLENGE CUP FINALS

HM QUEEN ELIZABETH II AND ERIC CLAY: WAKEFIELD TRINITY 38
HULL 5 AT WEMBLEY STADIUM, MIDDLESEX HA9 0WS ENGLAND.
3PM SATURDAY 14 MAY 1960. FEATHERSTONE ROVERS 17
BARROW 12 AT WEMBLEY STADIUM, EMPIRE WAY, MIDDLESEX
HA9 0WS ENGLAND. 3PM SATURDAY 13 MAY 1967.

There is no love lost between local rivals Wakefield Trinity and Featherstone Rovers but they do have one thing in common – they are the only two clubs to have won the Challenge Cup in front of the Queen. The Princess Royal clearly enjoyed watching Wigan beat Hull 30-13 in the 1959 final because her mother turned up the following year to see Wakefield Trinity beat Hull by the even wider margin of 38-5. And the Queen obviously enjoyed her visit because she repeated the experience just seven years later, becoming the last reigning British monarch to attend a Challenge Cup Final and the only one to attend two. By a remarkable coincidence referee Eric Clay (aka "the Sergeant Major"), who only officiated at two Challenge Cup finals, was in charge on both occasions.

DID YOU KNOW?

Having had the dubious distinction of being the first club to lose three successive Challenge Cup finals (from 1908-1910, in the days before the final was played at Wembley), Hull's 1960 defeat by Wakefield Trinity gave them the added distinction of being the first to lose two successive Wembley finals. (See also 1982)

FIRST
RUGBY LEAGUE FIXTURES ON SUNDAY

Bradford Northern 33 York 8 at Provident Stadium, Odsal, Bradford, West Yorkshire BD6 1BS England. Sunday 17 December 1967.
Leigh 15 Dewsbury 10 at Hilton Park, Leigh, Lancashire, England. Sunday 17 December 1967.

Rugby league was the first major sport to adopt Sunday as its main playing day in Britain. Attendances were dropping so it was decided to play on a Sunday but that laid the sport open to prosecution under the Sunday Observance Act of 1870. It was also problematic insofar as clubs could not charge for admission so spectators were let in if they bought a programme. In 1977, the Rugby Football League declared Sunday as its official match day.

ONLY

RUGBY UNION PLAYER TO
CAPTAIN WALES
BEFORE REACHING AGE OF 21

GARETH EDWARDS: WALES 5 SCOTLAND 0 AT CARDIFF ARMS PARK, WESTGATE STREET, CARDIFF CF10 1JA WALES. SATURDAY 3 FEBRUARY 1968.

Regarded by many as "arguably the greatest player ever to don a Welsh jersey", Gareth Owen Edwards won his first cap on April Fool's Day 1967 against France at Paris. Les Bleus won by 20-14. Ten months later and Edwards was handed the captaincy and won his first game in charge.

In 1969, Edwards was named Player of the Year in Wales. Five years later, he was named BBC Wales Sports Personality of the Year. He was a team captain on *A Question Of Sport* from 1979 until 1981 and in 2015 he was knighted in the Queen's Birthday Honours.

FIRST

RUGBY UNION REPLACEMENT

BARRY BRESNIHAN: BRITISH LIONS XV 20 WESTERN TRANSVAAL 12 AT POTCHEFSTROOM'S PROFERT OLIËN PARK, TRANSVAAL, SOUTH AFRICA. SATURDAY 18 MAY 1968.

Born at Waterford in 1944, Finbarr Patrick Kieran Bresnihan was capped twenty-five times as a centre for Ireland between 1966 and 1971. He replaced fellow Irishman Mike Gibson who damaged his ankle. Gibson would himself become the first replacement in Tests (see overleaf). Bresnihan died on 18 July 2010.

FIRST
INTERNATIONAL RUGBY UNION REPLACEMENT

MIKE GIBSON: BRITISH LIONS 20 SOUTH AFRICA 25 AT LOFTUS VERSFELD STADIUM, 440 KIRKNESS STREET, PRETORIA, GAUTENG, SOUTH AFRICA. SATURDAY 8 JUNE 1968.

Mike Gibson became the first official replacement in international rugby when he came on for the injured Barry John in the Lions' first Test against South Africa.

FIRST
RUGBY UNION REPLACEMENT FOR IRELAND

MICK HIPWELL: IRELAND 17 FRANCE 9 AT LANSDOWNE ROAD, BALLSBRIDGE, DUBLIN 4 REPUBLIC OF IRELAND. SATURDAY 25 JANUARY 1969.

Michael Louis Hipwell made his international debut at Twickenham on 10 February 1962 in a defeat by England. Seven years later, he became Ireland's first replacement when he came on for Noel Murphy as Ireland beat France.

FIRST
RUGBY UNION REPLACEMENT FOR ENGLAND

TIM DALTON: ENGLAND 8 SCOTLAND 3 AT TWICKENHAM STADIUM, WHITTON ROAD, TWICKENHAM, MIDDLESEX TW2 7BA ENGLAND. SATURDAY 15 MARCH 1969.

In the Calcutta Cup match, Dalton came on as a replacement for Keith Fielding who had suffered a twisted ankle. In 1968 the IRB had decreed that a replacement could be used but only after an independent doctor had examined the player and found that he was too poorly to continue.

FIRST

ROMAN CATHOLIC PRIEST TO PLAY
INTERNATIONAL RUGBY LEAGUE

Father John Cootes, Australia 20 New Zealand 10 at Carlaw Park,
Parnell, Auckland 1010, New Zealand. Sunday 1 June 1969.

In 1967 he began playing for Western Suburbs in the Newcastle rugby
league. Two years later, winger Father Cootes was picked for Australia's
tour of New Zealand and made his debut in the first Test scoring two
tries before a crowd of 13,459. He also played in the second Test of the
series. His **last Test match** was the final of the 1970 World Cup on 7
November, against Great Britain. He eventually left the priesthood and
opened a chain of furniture shops in New South Wales.

FIRST

ENGLAND RUGBY UNION COACH

DON WHITE, ENGLAND 11 SOUTH AFRICA 8 AT TWICKENHAM
STADIUM, WHITTON ROAD, TWICKENHAM, MIDDLESEX TW2 7BA
ENGLAND. 20 DECEMBER 1969

In its obituary after his death on 21 April 2007, *The Guardian* described
White as "one of the giants of English rugby during the golden years of
the amateur player". He made 448 appearances for Northampton before
retiring as a player in 1961 having served seven years as captain, but that
wasn't the end of his involvement in the game – eight years later, in
December 1969, he masterminded a victory for his country as England's
first coach. It was an auspicious start but unfortunately things didn't
continue as successfully, and in eleven matches over the next two seasons
he managed just two more wins and a draw.

DID YOU KNOW?

The match was played amid protests against the apartheid system
in South Africa. As the Springbok team was getting on board to
go to Twickenham a protester jumped in front of them, grabbed
the steering wheel of the coach and drove away. Some players
grabbed him and the coach crashed into six or so cars. It would
be the Springboks' last visit to Billy Williams's Cabbage Patch for
twenty-three years.

LAST

TIME BRITAIN WON THE
RUGBY LEAGUE ASHES

**Australia 17 Great Britain 21 at Sydney Cricket Ground,
Moore Park, Moore Park Road, Sydney, New South Wales
2021 Australia. Saturday 4 July 1970.**

The 1970 rugby league Lions were the most successful, winning twenty-two of their twenty-four games, drawing one and losing one. The loss was a crucial one, though – it was the first Test in Brisbane, which meant that they had to make sure of the second Test in Sydney, which they won 28-7 on 20 June. Two weeks later, in front of a crowd of 61,258 Britain managed to win the series by a mere four points – a narrow victory, and their last to date in an Ashes series.

FIRST

SPONSORED RUGBY LEAGUE WORLD CUP

ENGLAND. WEDNESDAY 21 OCTOBER-SATURDAY 7 NOVEMBER 1970.

The 1970 World Cup was the fourth tournament and the first one sponsored – by the Vehicle & General insurance group. The winners would be presented with the V&G Trophy rather than the World Cup with the original trophy being on display in a ceremonial capacity. The V&G Trophy was kept by the winners and never seen again. The Australian team, the holders, were staying at the Midland Hotel, Bradford, and the World Cup, which had cost eight million francs to make, was put on display. On 1 November it was stolen and remained hidden for twenty years. No one knows where it was kept during that period. Father-of-four Stephen Uttley discovered it among rubbish dumped in a ditch a few yards from the Bradford and Bingley Rugby League Club, Bingley, in April 1990. Mr Uttley did not realise its significance and telephoned local rugby clubs but no one was interested. He took the trophy into the local police station but after twenty-eight days it was returned to him. He rang Yorkshire TV's programme *Calendar* but their interest was not piqued either. Finally, he rang his local newspaper, *Telegraph & Argus*, and they ran a story on it. The World Cup was recognised by rugby league historian Trevor Delaney who finally ensured that on 1 June 1990 it was reunited with the Rugby Football League at Leeds. The World Cup was presented to the winners of the 2000 tournament (Australia).

LAST
ENGLAND TEST MATCH
AGAINST NON-NATIONAL OPPONENTS

ENGLAND 11 RUGBY FOOTBALL UNION PRESIDENT'S OVERSEAS XV 28 AT TWICKENHAM STADIUM, WHITTON ROAD, TWICKENHAM, MIDDLESEX TW2 7BA ENGLAND. SATURDAY 17 APRIL 1971.

England played a Rugby Football Union President's Overseas XV to commemorate the centenary of the Rugby Football Union. The players were selected from Australia, Fiji, France, New Zealand and South Africa. The attendance was 50,000. Of the fifteen who played, two – Stephen Knight of Australia and Wayne Cottrell of New Zealand – never represented their country in a full international against England.

FIRST
WELSH RUGBY UNION PLAYER
TO CAPTAIN BRITISH LIONS

JOHN DAWES: BRITISH LIONS 9 ALL BLACKS 3 AT CARISBROOK STADIUM, MURRAYFIELD STREET, SOUTH DUNEDIN, DUNEDIN 9012, NEW ZEALAND. SATURDAY 26 JUNE 1971.

Sydney John Dawes was born in the summer of 1940 and played for Newbridge in Monmouthshire before joining London Welsh and making his debut for Wales in 1964 playing against Ireland. He was picked for the **Welsh rugby team's first overseas tour** the same year and played in **Wales's first match outside of Europe** and its **first in the southern hemisphere** – against East Africa in Nairobi, Kenya, on 12 May 1964. He made twenty-two appearances for his country, captaining the side in six of them, including leading the Grand Slam-winning side of 1971. He played four times for the British Lions, all on the tour to New Zealand when he was captain – the **only time a Lions team won a series in New Zealand**.

> ## DID YOU KNOW?
> The British Lions won the first Test, lost the second and won the third before tying the fourth to give them victory. However, if the scoring system in place today had been in situ in 1971, they would have lost 18-16.

FIRST
WINNERS OF RUGBY LEAGUE
PLAYER'S NO 6 TROPHY
(LATER JOHN PLAYER TROPHY, LATER JOHN PLAYER SPECIAL TROPHY, LATER REGAL TROPHY) HALIFAX 22 WAKEFIELD TRINITY 11 AT ODSAL STADIUM, ODSAL, BRADFORD, WEST YORKSHIRE. BD6 1BS ENGLAND. 2.30PM SATURDAY 22 JANUARY 1972.

In the same season that cigarette manufacturers John Player & Son sponsored rugby union's first national knockout competition (see following entry) they also introduced a new knockout competition to rugby league, open to thirty professional clubs and the two top amateur sides. Although it never achieved the prestige of the Challenge Cup the trophy has produced some memorable shocks, such as second division Blackpool Borough's unlikely appearance in the 1977 final (their only appearance in any cup final), amateurs Cawoods (of Hull) beating Halifax 9-8 in the first round of the 1977/78 competition, and Castleford's thirty-one-point victory over Wigan in 1994 at odds of 1/125. Halifax were the inaugural winners.

FIRST
BRITISH RUGBY UNION
NATIONAL KNOCKOUT COMPETITION
Rugby Football Union Club Competition. 1971-1972

The Rugby Football Union Club Competition began in the 1971-1972 season and was won by Gloucester who beat Moseley 17-6 in the final. Coventry won the competition two years in a row in 1972/73 and 1973/74. It was renamed the John Player Cup in 1976. In 2006 **Welsh teams entered for the first time**.

FIRST
BLACK PLAYER TO CAPTAIN A
BRITISH NATIONAL TEAM
IN ANY SPORT (RUGBY LEAGUE)

FIRST
RUGBY LEAGUE PLAYER TO
FEATURE ON *THIS IS YOUR LIFE*

LAST
BRITISH RUGBY LEAGUE CAPTAIN
TO LIFT THE WORLD CUP

ONLY
RUGBY LEAGUE PLAYER
TO HAVE A DUAL CARRIAGEWAY
AND A PLAY NAMED AFTER HIM

CLIVE SULLIVAN, MBE: GREAT BRITAIN 10 FRANCE 9 AT STADE MUNICIPAL, 1 ALLÉE GABRIEL BIÉNÈS, 31028 TOULOUSE, FRANCE. SUNDAY 6 FEBRUARY 1972

Born in Cardiff on 9 April 1943, Sullivan overcame heavy odds to become a star rugby league player. Injuries and illness meant that by his early teens he had had a number of operations on his knees, feet and shoulders but his perseverance was rewarded by a trial with Bradford Northern at the age of 17. Bradford Northern turned him down but Hull had the foresight to play him in the first team on 9 December 1961 as an unnamed trialist – and after he scored a hat-trick on that first appearance they signed him the following day. He became Hull's captain and coach, and scored 247 tries in 337 appearances for the club over the next twelve and a quarter years. He made a scoring Great Britain debut in 1967 and took over the captaincy in 1972, becoming the first black captain of any

British national team in any sport. He scored in both that year's Tests against France and then went on to captain Great Britain to victory in the 1972 World Cup, scoring a try in each of Britain's four games, including a length of the field try to level the final 10-10 against Australia for Britain's last World Cup victory to date. (When the final remained level after extra time Britain won the cup having finished top of the table in the qualifying rounds.) That same year Sully became the first rugby league player to feature on the television programme *This Is Your Life*, and in the 1974 New Year's Honours List he was awarded the MBE. Two months later, he resigned as Hull coach and transferred to local rivals Hull Kingston Rovers, for whom he scored 118 tries in 213 games, culminating in Rovers' victory over Hull in the 1980 Challenge Cup Final (see 1980). Meanwhile his international career continued with three Tests for Great Britain against Australia and captaining Wales to third place in the 1975 World Cup. After leaving Hull KR he spent a year on loan to Oldham before returning to Hull FC and gaining a second Challenge Cup winner's medal in the 1982 replay against Widnes (see 1982). He died of cancer just three years later, at the age of 42. In his honour, the A63 dual carriageway, which passes under the landmark Humber Bridge, was renamed Clive Sullivan Way.

<hr/>

LAST
TEST MATCH OF BARRY JOHN
Five Nations Championship: Wales 20 France 6
at Cardiff Arms Park, Westgate Street, Cardiff
CF10 1JA Wales. Saturday 25 March 1972.

Barry John was one of the heroes of Welsh rugby. His final international was at home to France and in the match he converted four penalty goals and in scoring his final penalty surpassed the Wales international points scoring record of Jack Bancroft set nearly 60 years earlier. At the age of 27, with twenty-five Wales caps and five British Lions ones under his belt John announced his retirement. He won ninety points comprising five tries, nine conversions, thirteen penalties and eight dropped goals.

LAST

OF RUGBY LEAGUE
FOUR-TACKLE RULE IN BRITAIN

LEEDS 9 SWINTON 5 AT STATION ROAD, PENDLEBURY,
MANCHESTER, ENGLAND. SATURDAY 20 MAY 1972.

The change of possession after six tackles is one of the distinguishing features of rugby league, creating the rhythm and structure of the game. But it is only a relatively recent innovation. For more than seventy years a team could retain possession indefinitely, but this allowed teams to play unadventurous "stick it up your jumper" rugby in order not to lose the ball, so in 1966 the Rugby Football League introduced a four-tackle rule, with a scrum being formed after a team had been tackled four times. The four-tackle rule was adopted in Australia and New Zealand the following year – legend has it that one of the reasons for its adoption was in an attempt to end St George's stranglehold on the Sydney Premiership (see 1966). However, four tackles made for a staccato game with not enough opportunity for teams to develop attacking moves, so at the beginning of the 1972/73 season six tackles were adopted instead. The last British game of rugby league under the four-tackle rule was the 1971/72 Championship Final between Leeds and Swinton. The six-tackle rule was agreed internationally in 1976, and in 1983 the sixth-tackle scrum was replaced by a hand-over of possession to the defending team, making the game faster and yet more exciting.

FIRST

RUGBY LEAGUE PLAYER TO RECEIVE A
CHALLENGE CUP WINNER'S MEDAL
AND A SYDNEY GRAND FINAL
WINNER'S MEDAL

MALCOLM REILLY: CASTLEFORD (SATURDAY 17
MAY 1969 AND SATURDAY 9 MAY 1970) AND MANLY-
WARRINGAH (SATURDAY 16 SEPTEMBER 1972 AND
SATURDAY 15 SEPTEMBER 1973).

Loose forward Malcolm Reilly was one of rugby league's hard men, but he was also one of the best ball handlers on either side of the world. He was instrumental in Britain's last Ashes victory to date (see 1970), in Manly's first Sydney Premiership and its retention the following year, and (as player and coach) in securing eleven of the nineteen trophies in Castleford's history to date. He appears in Castleford's greatest fantasy team, and in 2006 he was voted in as the only Pom in Manly's greatest team. Reilly signed for Castleford in 1965, and the club won a trophy a year for the next five years (see 1965), including two consecutive Challenge Cups in 1969 and 1970. His performance in the first of those Challenge Cup wins, an 11-6 victory over Salford, was summed up by one newspaper as: "Reilly, the Lance Todd winner, really was superb, his burst through broken fields, his determination to fend off tackles and, having done so, his cleverness in getting the ball away contributed to Salford's downfall."

His storming performance in the 1970 Ashes series prompted Manly (sadly for Castleford and Great Britain) to pay him a then world record £15,000 to emigrate to Australia, where he made a similar impact on the Sea Eagles as he had on Castleford: in his first season (1971) Manly won the minor premiership, and in his second and third they won the first two major Premierships in the club's history. Reilly thus became the first player to receive a Challenge Cup winner's medal and a Sydney Grand Final winner's medal. In the second of his Grand Finals Reilly was involved in an infamous brawl with Souths forward George Piggins, who later wrote in his book *Never Say Die*: "Malcolm was a very tough player, and a bloody good one. Manly paid a fortune to bring him from England, and he gave them value, despite hobbling on a crook knee for much of the time. Anyone who tries to tell you that Englishmen aren't tough… forget it."

DID YOU KNOW?

One of Malcolm Reilly's coaching protégés, Kevin Ward, emulated Reilly's feat in 1986 and 1987 with the same two clubs: Ward propped for Castleford in their Challenge Cup victory over Hull Kingston Rovers (see 1986) and for Manly in their Grand Final victory over Canberra (see 1987).

ONLY

FIVE-WAY TIE IN THE
RUGBY UNION
FIVE NATIONS TOURNAMENT
FIVE NATIONS: SATURDAY 13 JANUARY-SATURDAY 14 APRIL 1973.

This was the only time that all five countries finished on four points having all won two and lost two matches. Had the competition been decided on point difference then Wales would have come first (plus ten) followed by Ireland and France jointly on plus two, Scotland (minus four) and England (minus ten) taking home the wooden spoon. If it had been decided on most points scored then Scotland (55) would have been champions and Wales (53) runners-up.

ONLY

ENGLAND RUGBY TOUR CANCELLED
BECAUSE OF A KIDNAP THREAT
England to Argentina. Summer 1973.

In the summer of 1973, England were due to tour Argentina but had to cancel after Peronist groups made threats to kidnap the team. Instead, England toured New Zealand and Fiji.

FIRST

STREAKER AT A RUGBY
FOOTBALL MATCH (RUGBY UNION)
MICHAEL O'BRIEN, "THE ONE WITH THE POLICEMAN'S HELMET": ENGLAND 7 FRANCE 26 AT TWICKENHAM STADIUM, WHITTON ROAD, TWICKENHAM, MIDDLESEX TW2 7BA ENGLAND. SATURDAY 20 APRIL 1974

On 3 March 1974, a Turkish DC-10 crashed into woods north-east of Paris killing 346 people, including rugby fans travelling back from the Five Nations match in Paris. A charity match was arranged to raise funds for what was then the world's worst air crash but the match is remembered for reasons other than sport. Australian stockbroker Michael O'Brien "arrived at the ground early, and had a few drinks" and then "My mates were talking about how impossible it would be to streak across the park. But a few drinks later I said it could be done. My friends surrounded me and I stripped off. Two of them went across to the other side of the terracing and waited there with my clothes. When the half-time whistle went I just ran out." The classic photograph of the 26-year-old shows him with long hair and beard and his arms outstretched in the even longer arms of the law. Twenty years later he said: "I quite honestly thought I'd get to the other side of the oval, get dressed and disappear into the crowd without anybody ever knowing it was me." Instead, he found himself with a £10 fine (imposed by Richmond magistrates for "insulting behaviour") and no job, but at least he won the £10 bet – streaking has since spread to a number of other sports, from football and cricket to indoor bowls. As for the helmet, PC Bruce Perry said: "I feared he would be mobbed, or that other people would follow suit. I felt embarrassed so I covered him up as best I could. It was a cold day – he had nothing to be proud of. I didn't know what to say so I gave him the caution: 'You are not obliged to say anything unless you wish to do so, etc etc,' and… he turns around and says 'Give us a kiss'."

• • •••• •

FIRST
RUGBY LEAGUE PLAYER TO CAPTAIN
THREE DIFFERENT CLUBS TO
CHALLENGE CUP VICTORY AT WEMBLEY

ALEX MURPHY: ST HELENS, LEIGH AND WARRINGTON, WARRINGTON 24 FEATHERSTONE ROVERS 9 AT WEMBLEY STADIUM, EMPIRE WAY, MIDDLESEX HA9 0WS ENGLAND. SATURDAY 11 MAY 1974.

Alex Murphy played for three clubs, and captained all three of them to victory at Wembley. He signed for his hometown club, St Helens, at one minute past midnight on 22 April 1955 – his sixteenth birthday – and three years later, in 1958, he beat Billy Boston's record as the youngest British Lion (see 1954). On the international stage he made his name as the best scrum half in the world, starting with an awesome performance in the "Rorke's Drift Test" (see 1958), and at home he won every trophy there was to win.

He won the Challenge Cup twice with St Helens, scoring a try in Saints' 12-6 victory over Wigan in 1966 and a captain's drop-goal in the last two minutes of the 21-2 victory over the same club six years later.

The following year he controversially left St Helens after a disagreement, and four years after that he was once again lifting the Challenge Cup at Wembley as captain-coach of Leigh. This time he scored two drop-goals and took the Lance Todd Trophy for his part in Leigh's 24-7 demolition of the outright favourites, Leeds, a performance summed up by the press: "Gifted with that inestimable quality of bringing the best out in others by example, he was the scourge of Leeds in this game."

Controversial as ever, he left Leigh immediately after the final to take up the reins as captain-coach at Warrington, and three years later he was lifting the cup yet again, this time after scoring two drop-goals in the 24-9 defeat of the holders, Featherstone Rovers.

Asked whom he considered to be the best player in the world, "Murphy the Mouth" replied with his typical brashness, "Apart from me, you mean?"

DID YOU KNOW?

During Leigh's 15 May 1971 Challenge Cup victory, Leeds captain and centre Syd Hynes became **the first man to be sent off at Wembley**, in somewhat controversial circumstances. Midway through the second half the two captains appeared to clash in midfield and Murphy was left motionless on the turf. Referee W.H. Thompson sent off Hynes for butting and Murphy was stretchered off to the dressing room, only to return minutes later and play out the rest of the match, apparently undamaged.

ONLY
WINNERS OF RUGBY LEAGUE
CAPTAIN MORGAN TROPHY

ONLY
WINNERS OF RUGBY LEAGUE
CLUB CHAMPIONSHIP

**Warrington 4 Featherstone Rovers 0 at The Willows, Willows Road,
Salford, Lancashire M5 5FQ England. Saturday 26 January 1974
and Warrington 13 St Helens 12 at Central Park, Central Park Way,
Wigan, Lancashire WN1 1XS England. Saturday 18 May 1974.**

In the 1973/74 season, Seagram's sponsored a rugby league knockout
competition under the name of their Captain Morgan brand of rum,
named after the 17th century Welsh pirate, Captain Henry Morgan.
The competition, which was open to the sixteen first-round winners
of the Yorkshire and Lancashire Cups, lasted only one season, with
Warrington as the only winners (both Captain Morgan finalists failed
to reach the final of their respective County Cups). That same season
the Rugby Football League experimented with an end of season Club
Championship knockout competition to replace the top 16 play-offs
– that, too, lasted only one season and was also won by Warrington.

FIRST
ENGLAND TEST PLAYER SENT OFF

MIKE BURTON: ENGLAND 21 AUSTRALIA 30 AT BALLYMORE
STADIUM, 91 CLYDE ROAD, HERSTON, QUEENSLAND 4006
AUSTRALIA. SATURDAY 31 MAY 1975.

Prop forward Mike Burton made his debut in the Gloucester front row
on 14 November 1964 when he was 18. It was the first of what would be
360 appearances for the club. He first played for England in 1972 against
Wales. He toured New Zealand in 1973 and two years later while touring
Australia he became the first Englishman to be sent off at international

level. It was in the second Test (later nicknamed the Battle of Brisbane) that Burton was sent off just three minutes into the match by Bob Burnett, a local Queensland referee, for a late tackle on the Australian winger Doug Osborne.

ONLY
RUGBY UNION INTERNATIONAL
KILLED BY LIGHTNING
DURING A FIRST CLASS MATCH

JEAN-FRANÇOIS PHLIPONEAU: STADE MARCEL-MICHELIN, 35 RUE DU CLOS-FOUR, 63100 CLERMONT-FERRAND, FRANCE. SATURDAY 8 MAY 1976.

Phliponeau played two games on the wing for France, on 24 March 1973 against Wales and on 14 April 1973 against Ireland (see 1973). Three years later, on 8 May 1976, he was playing for his club Montferrand in a triangular meeting with Vichy and Aurillac when he was struck by lightning. His wife, Annick, was watching in the stands. The 25-year-old died of his injuries the following day.

FIRST
STREAKER AT A RUGBY LEAGUE
CHALLENGE CUP FINAL

THE "WEMBLEY CONDUCTOR": ST HELENS 20 WIDNES 5 AT WEMBLEY STADIUM, EMPIRE WAY, MIDDLESEX HA9 0WS ENGLAND. SATURDAY 8 MAY 1976.

Purists do not count the Wembley Conductor as a streaker because he retained his modesty by keeping on his socks and boxer shorts, but he did manage to climb onto the crossbar, from where he conducted the military band and then meekly climbed down to be arrested.

FIRST

IRISH PLAYER
SENT OFF IN A TEST

FIRST

WELSH PLAYER SENT OFF
IN A TEST

**WILLIE DUGGAN (IRELAND) AND GEOFF WHEEL
(WALES): WALES 25 IRELAND 9 AT CARDIFF ARMS
PARK, WESTGATE STREET, CARDIFF CF10 1JA WALES.
SATURDAY 15 JANUARY 1977.**

Ireland No 8 Duggan became the first player dismissed for fighting when he got involved in a brawl with Wales lock Geoff Wheel at the Arms Park. Scottish referee Norman Sansom sent off both players although Duggan was later to claim that he had not been sent off in the usually accepted manner. The late Moss Keane revealed: "Willie said to me that the referee came towards him and said would he mind leaving the field? And Duggan says: 'Sure, not at all'. 'I was buggered anyway'."

ONLY

BLUE PETER PRESENTER TO SHARE A
BATH WITH FUTURE GREAT BRITAIN
RUGBY LEAGUE COACH MALCOLM REILLY

John Noakes: Noakes's Nomads 13 Castleford 19 at Wheldon Road, Castleford, West Yorkshire, WF10 2SD England. Autumn 1977

John Noakes hails from Halifax, but it was Castleford who took up *Blue Peter*'s invitation to stage an exhibition match in which the plucky presenter, who had played rugby union at school, could show off his skills as a scrum half. Noakes's choice of position raised the eyebrows of BBC commentator Eddie Waring, who told him just before kick-off: "Well, you've got some courage, I'll say that. When Mal Reilly comes round that pack you'll need to get a bit of a move on." But Waring was less impressed when Noakes flung himself onto the ground as he made his first pass: "John Noakes is giving us a rugby *union* pass!" Union or not, the pass found Dennis Hartley who set up a move which ended with future England coach John Kear passing to Noakes, who side-stepped some theatrically lax tackling to score. After the match Eddie Waring summed up Noakes's effort: "…he stayed to the end, he scored a try and he got a goal. But I'll bet he's looking forward to the solace of the bath." Noakes got to sit at the tap end, next to Malcolm Reilly.

LAST
TEST MATCH OF GARETH EDWARDS

WALES 16 FRANCE 7 AT CARDIFF ARMS PARK, WESTGATE STREET, CARDIFF CF10 1JA WALES. SATURDAY 18 MARCH 1978

Gareth Edwards played his fifty-third and last game for Wales against the country with whom it all began although this time he was on the winning side and at the headquarters of Welsh rugby. That year, Wales also won the Grand Slam and became **the first team to win three consecutive Triple Crowns**. To add to his achievements Edwards was named Rothmans Player of the Year for 1978.

FIRST
GRAND SLAM BY THE ALL BLACKS

LAST
"GREAT FOLK MEMORY"

ONLY
RUGBY UNION TEAM TO BEAT THE ALL BLACKS ON THE "GRAND SLAM" TOUR

ONLY
SINGLE MATCH TO HAVE BOTH A
PLAY AND A BOOK WRITTEN ABOUT IT

**MUNSTER 12 ALL BLACKS 0 AT THOMOND PARK,
CRATLOE ROAD, LIMERICK, REPUBLIC OF IRELAND.
3PM TUESDAY 31 OCTOBER 1978.**

The 1978 All Blacks achieved what no others had done before – the first Grand Slam, beating all four Home Countries and the Barbarians. They played eighteen games on that tour and won all but one – and that one is so legendary that Irish playwright James Breen described it as "the last great folk memory". Part of the reason for the match's mythical status is that Irish television broadcaster RTE was opening a second channel a few days later and was too busy to send an outside broadcast unit to the match, so the memory has been passed down by word of mouth; and through Breen's play *Alone It Stands* and Arthur English's book *Stand Up And Fight*.

The All Blacks arrived at Thomond Park brimming with confidence after victories against Cambridge, Cardiff, West Wales and London Counties but that confidence was severely dented by the ferocity of Munster's defence, particularly a bone-crunching tackle by Seamus Dennison on Stu Wilson just minutes after kick-off. After just nine minutes Munster led 6-0 from a converted try, and a drop goal gave them a 9-0 half-time lead. Munster then withstood the inevitable fight back before scoring another drop goal eleven minutes from time to seal the Irish folk memory. Afterwards, All Blacks coach Graham Mourie said: "They played the type of game we tried to play, but they played it better."

DID YOU KNOW?

Legend has it that when the All Blacks played the Barbarians in the final match of the tour on 16 December 1978 Munster fans were the only people in Great Britain and the Republic of Ireland desperately hoping that the All Blacks would win, thus leaving Munster as the only team to have beaten the tourists: their wish was granted (18-16), giving the All Blacks a historic first and Munster a legendary only.

ONLY

RUGBY LEAGUE PLAYER
TO MAKE SIX REPRESENTATIVE
TRIPS DOWN UNDER

Roger "the Dodger" Millward, Hull Kingston Rovers. June 1979

At 5ft 4in and weighing only ten stone, Millward was not the archetypal rugby league player, but his speed and agile side-step soon caught the eye of the Great Britain selection panel and led Eddie Waring to dub him "Roger the Dodger". The Hull Kingston Rovers website describes him as "easily the best player to pull on the famous red and white Hull Kingston Rovers shirt and possibly the best player to ever wear the Great Britain shirt" – and despite the possibility of bias from the Robins' website, few would argue with that. He made his Test debut on 5 March 1966 at the age of just eighteen and transferred from Castleford to Hull Kingston Rovers for £6,000 (£103,000 at 2015 values) on 8 August the same year, going on to make 413 appearances for the Robins and to become the most successful coach in the club's history.

His first taste of Australasia came in the disastrous World Cup campaign of 1968, but two years later he made up for the disappointment by starring in Great Britain's last Ashes win over Australia (see 1970) – omitted from the team for the first Test, which Britain lost, he scored twenty of Britain's twenty-eight points in the second, and "strode onto a pass from Doug Laughton and set sail for the corner at the Sydney Cricket Ground" to score the try that sealed victory in the third. He toured with the Lions again in 1974 and 1979, and captained England in the 1975 World Championship in Australia and Great Britain in the 1977 World Cup, in which GB came within one point of victory, losing 13-12 to Australia in Sydney. That same year Millward took over as coach at Hull Kingston Rovers, and as captain-coach led the club to every major honour in the game. In 1983, he was awarded the MBE for services to rugby league and to sport in Britain.

DID YOU KNOW?

In Millward's last senior game as a player he became the only captain to receive the Challenge Cup from the late Queen Elizabeth. It was one of Wembley's most famous finals, in which two of the game's closest rivals did battle: Hull FC and Hull Kingston Rovers. Legend has it that as the entire city decamped to Wembley for the final, one wag spray-painted a road bridge on the A63 with the sign: "Last one out turn off the lights". In the thirteenth minute of the final Hull hooker Ron Wileman broke Millward's jaw in a late, high tackle but Millward had the last laugh, staying on the field and leading the Robins to a well-deserved victory. Hull Kingston Rovers fans still taunt Hull FC fans with the scoreline 10-5.

FIRST

TEAM TO BE
SECOND DIVISION CHAMPIONS TWICE

ONLY

FIRST CLASS BRITISH RUGBY LEAGUE TEAM
TO WIN ALL ITS GAMES IN A SEASON

HULL FC. ENGLAND. FRIDAY 18 MAY 1979.

At the end of the 1972/73 season the rugby league changed from a one division to a two divison structure. Having finished in the bottom half of the table that season, Hull found themselves in Division Two. They narrowly missed promotion (on points difference) in 1975/76 and achieved it in 1976/77 but were relegated again in 1977/78 after just one season in the top flight.

The following season they broke all records by becoming the only first class team to win all its games in a season, winning all 26 games with 702 points for and just 175 against.

LAST
WINNERS OF RUGBY LEAGUE
BBC2 FLOODLIT TROPHY

Hull FC 13 Hull Kingston Rovers 3 at The Boulevard Stadium, Kingston upon Hull, East Riding of Yorkshire, England. Tuesday 18 December 1979.

The last club to win the trophy was Hull FC, who beat neighbours Hull Kingston Rovers 13-3 at home in front of a crowd of 18,500 – by far the biggest crowd in the fourteen years of the competition.

FIRST
RUGBY LEAGUE
STATE OF ORIGIN WINNER

QUEENSLAND 20 NEW SOUTH WALES 10 AT LANG PARK, 40 CASTLEMAINE STREET, MILTON, QUEENSLAND 4064 AUSTRALIA. TUESDAY 8 JULY 1980.

The Australian State of Origin series, billed as "State against state; mate against mate", is universally recognised as the toughest series of rugby league matches in the world. Interstate rugby matches had been played in Australia even before the schism (see 1908), and continued after the establishment of the Australian rugby league, but until 1979 each state selected players from the clubs in that state, regardless of the players' origin. As more and more Queenslanders "emigrated" to play in the Sydney Premiership, New South Wales grew stronger and stronger until the interstate series became a mockery and the Australian rugby league decided to try an idea already pioneered in Australian Rules football in 1977 – selection would be based on the state in which a player made his senior debut, rather than the state in which he was playing at the time. In 1980, after Queensland had predictably lost two matches under the old selection rules, a State of Origin match was announced. The New South Wales media rubbished the idea as a "three day wonder" and Australian captain Bob Fulton dismissed it as "the non-event of the century" but a sell-out crowd of 33,210 people thought otherwise, and crammed into Lang Park to watch Queensland convincingly win the inaugural State of Origin match. The following year followed the same pattern: Queensland lost two games under the old selection rules and won the third under State of Origin selection rules, the third game generating so much interest that all three fixtures have been played as a State of Origin Series ever since. Queensland won each of the first three series by two to one, and New South Wales did not secure their inaugural series victory until 1985.

LAST
COMMENTARY BY EDDIE WARING

HULL KINGSTON ROVERS 11 HULL 7 AT HEADINGLEY, LEEDS, WEST YORKSHIRE LS6 3BU ENGLAND. SATURDAY 16 MAY 1981

To many he was the voice of rugby league in much the way Bill McLaren was the voice of rugby union although he did not find universal favour among fans. Like many football managers who were not gifted players, Edward Marsden Waring was not a top rugby player. Indeed, he had a trial with Nottingham Forest as a centre forward and once scored ten goals in a match. A brief stint as a journalist ended when in 1934 he became the youngest manager of Dewsbury RFC and they won the Championship in 1942 and the Challenge Cup in 1943 under his watch. Deafness in one ear prevented his call-up to the Army in the Second World War. After the war, he returned to journalism and covered the first post-war tour to Australia in 1946.

He liked to infer that he was the first to cover overseas matches but he was one of several on that trip but such was his talent for self-promotion that the others are forgotten. He persuaded the BBC to cover rugby league on Saturday afternoons and began commentating in 1951 and from 1958 on *Grandstand*. It began a career that lasted thirty years although in 1976, there were calls for Waring to go, the fans unaware that the commentator was showing the first signs of Alzheimer's disease. On 11 May 1968 in the Challenge Cup Final at Wembley, Waring commentated as Wakefield Trinity's Don Fox (1935-2008) missed his conversion kick in front of the posts, handing the game to Leeds 11-10. Waring's speech became the "They think it's all over…" of rugby: "He's missed it, he's missed it! He's on the ground… he's missed it! Well, and there goes the whistle for time. What a dramatic… everybody's got their head in their hands… and he's sure in tears, he's in tears is the poor lad." It is said that, on the day after the match, Waring accompanied Fox to the Featherstone Rovers ground, where the Wakefield player kicked several goals wearing a pair of carpet slippers. Waring became known for his stock phrases "He's gone for an early bath" when a player was sent off, "It's an up and under!" and "You're looking at one ton of rugby – meat, brawn, muscle, brain, the lot of it!" On 11 May 1969 Waring recorded his first *It's A Knockout* alongside David Vine and referee Arthur Ellis. Waring left the show in 1981, a year before it ended having co-presented since 1972 with Stuart Hall. On 2 May 1981 he commentated on his last Challenge Cup Final (Widnes beat Hull Kingston Rovers 18-9 at Wembley) and on 16 May he gave his last rugby commentary at the end of season Premiership Final at Leeds in an all-Humberside final between Hull Kingston Rovers and Hull, which Hull Kingston Rovers won by 11-7. His closing words were, "So there it is... back to David Coleman in the *Grandstand* studio... it's all yours, David lad." Coleman said, "The television presentation of the match was by Nick Hunter, summaries were by Alex Murphy and, for the last time in *Grandstand*, we say the commentator was... Eddie Waring."

FIRST
BLACK RUGBY UNION SPRINGBOK

ERROL TOBIAS, SOUTH AFRICA 23 IRELAND 15 AT NEWLANDS STADIUM, 146 CAMPGROUND ROAD, NEWLANDS, CAPE TOWN 7700 SOUTH AFRICA. SATURDAY 30 MAY 1981.

One day in 1962, 12-year-old Errol George Tobias and his brother walked past a school in apartheid South Africa and stopped to watch the white boys practising rugby. One of the boys dropped the ball and Tobias remembers the teacher yelling: "You will never become a Springbok if you cannot catch the ball properly." Then Tobias's brother looked at him and said, "You are a Springbok... you never drop the ball." The brothers didn't know what a Springbok was. When their mother explained it she told them that coloured boys were not allowed to be Springboks, but Tobias remembered only the teacher's words: "If you could catch the ball you could become a Springbok. That's what the teacher had said." He persevered and proved to be a remarkable player, touring Britain with a coloured South African team in 1971 and representing the Barbarians in 1979. It was enough to catch the selectors' eyes, and on 30 May 1981 he pulled on the coveted green and gold to become the first black Springbok:

"As soon as I touched the ball I was showing that coloured people are good enough to play. I was giving coloured people the chance to have the honour to wear the blazer of South Africa." He played two Tests at centre that year and four more at fly half in 1984 – and during his four matches at fly half South Africa achieved a try-scoring rate which they never matched before or since. He later became a bricklayer and on 8 November 1995 was elected the first black mayor of his hometown of Caledon.

LAST

RUGBY LEAGUE CHALLENGE CUP
FINAL REPLAY

HULL 18 WIDNES 9 AT ELLAND ROAD, LEEDS, WEST YORKSHIRE LS11 0ES ENGLAND 7.30PM WEDNESDAY 19 MAY 1982.

There have only been three Challenge Cup Final replays, and Hull were involved in two of them. The first was in 1910, when Leeds beat Hull 26-23 at Huddersfield, and the second was Warrington's victory over Halifax in 1954 (see 1954). After the 14-14 draw between Widnes and Hull at Wembley in 1982, Hull coach Arthur Bunting said: "I think Widnes were lucky the final hooter went when it did." The outcome of the replay proved him right: Widnes took an early lead, as they had done at Wembley, but Hull's determination kept them in the game and shortly before half-time they took the lead for the first time in 113 minutes of play – although Widnes reduced the deficit to just four points, Hull held on for their first Challenge Cup in sixty-eight years.

DID YOU KNOW?

The 1982 replay was Hull's second Challenge Cup victory, having beaten Wakefield Trinity 6-0 at Halifax in 1914, before Wembley was built. Ever since the replay at Elland Road rival Hull Kingston Rovers fans have taunted Hull FC fans with the chant: "You'll never win at Wembley." To the delight of Hull Kingston Rovers fans, when Hull did win the Challenge Cup for a third time, beating Leeds Rhinos 25-24 in 2005, the final was played at the Millennium Stadium in Cardiff, while Wembley was being rebuilt.

LAST

SUBBUTEO TABLE RUGBY TEAM

R37 Widnes. England. 1983.

In August 1946, ornithologist Peter Adolph (1916/94) filed a patent for a game of table soccer that he wanted to call "The Hobby", a pun on a breed of falcon known as the Eurasian Hobby. When he was told that he couldn't register that name as a trademark he instead named the game after part of the bird's Latin name, *Falco subbuteo*, and a legend was born. During the 1950s Subbuteo branched out from soccer into cricket and rugby – league and union, although there were far more league than union teams produced. In the first version of Subbuteo table rugby the players were represented by flat tokens similar to draughts, with a picture of a player on a card insert which were rolled towards the try line. Then, *c.*1968/69, 00 scale players on hemispherical bases brought table rugby into the age of "flick to kick" (or in this case, flick to pass). The first 00 rugby team featured (by catalogue number, R1) had an amber/gold shirt and black shorts, and was a cross-code mix, being listed as "Australia or Bramley". R2 was England or Swansea, in white shirt and shorts. Subbuteo rugby was phased out – along with cricket and hockey – in 1983, the last team represented being R37 Widnes, in white shirt and black shorts.

ONLY

PLAYER TO REPRESENT THREE COUNTRIES

ENRIQUE EDGARDO: ARGENTINA, TAHITI AND AUSTRALIA. SATURDAY 9 JUNE 1984.

More than fifty players have played Tests for two countries but only one has pulled on the shirt of three countries. Enrique Edgardo Rodríguez was born in Argentina in 1952 and began playing rugby at Universidad Nacional de Córdoba in 1971. He made his Test debut for Argentina in 1979 against New Zealand and played thirteen times for his country.

On 14 July 1981, he represented Tahiti in an invitation game against France to celebrate Bastille Day. His last match for Argentina was against Australia on 7 August 1983 at the Sydney Cricket Ground. He liked Sydney so much that seven months later he emigrated there. Three months after that he was selected for Australia and on 9 June 1984, he made his debut for Australia against Fiji. His twenty-sixth and last Test for Australia was on 7 November 1987, ironically, against Argentina at Buenos Aires. He retired not long after his final Test and was diagnosed with manic depression.

ONLY
RUGBY LEAGUE CLUB NAMED AFTER A LAGER
Mansfield Marksman 35 Runcorn Hornets 6
at Athletic Grounds, Milnrow Road, Rochdale,
Lancashire, England. Sunday 2 September 1984.

Founded in 1984 at Mansfield, they played at Mansfield Town's Field Mill in the Second Division. They were sponsored by Mansfield Brewery and named Marksman after the brewery's lager. The side was predominantly made up of West Yorkshire-based players who travelled south to play. They won their first home (before 2,291 spectators on 9 September 1984) and away matches and won eight of their first nine games; the only defeat being 7-6 at Dewsbury. Then a decline began and they found it difficult to attract crowds. In the first year Mansfield Marksman lost £90,000 and could not afford to pay the rent to Mansfield Town. The last game at Field Mill was on 2 February 1986 when Marksman lost 32-2 to Leigh. The club moved to Alfreton Town's North Street stadium and on 23 March 1986 lost their first game there 42-18 to Workington Town in front of just 290 spectators.

The club moved again for the 1988/89 season taking up residence at Sutton Town's Lowmoor Road ground at Kirkby-in-Ashfield. In June 1989, the club faced a boardroom split and Mansfield Brewery pulled out of the sponsorship deal. The club was renamed Nottingham City RLFC. Relegated to the National Conference League in 1992/93, they went down in their first year and then resigned from the league the following year.

LAST

TIME HULL AND HULL KINGSTON ROVERS
MET IN THE YORKSHIRE CUP FINAL

HULL 29 HULL KINGSTON ROVERS 12 AT BOOTHFERRY PARK, HULL HU4 6EU ENGLAND. 3PM SATURDAY 27 OCTOBER 1984.

The two Humberside rivals may have only met once in the Challenge Cup Final (see June 1979 Did You Know?) but they have met three times in the Yorkshire Cup Final. The first was on 27 November 1920, when 20,000 people watched Hull Kingston Rovers win 2-0 at Headingley. The second was on 14 October 1967, when 16,729 watched Hull Kingston Rovers win, again at Headingley, by the even narrower margin of 8-7. Having halved the deficit between the first two clashes, Hull must have thought that 1984 would be third time lucky, and so it was. Moving the final to Hull City's ground boosted the crowd to 25,243 and made it a truly Humberside affair – the guest of honour was Kingston upon Hull's Lady Mayor who, far from remaining impartial, arrived completely bedecked in black and white. Her concession to mayoral balance was that her consort (who happened to be her daughter-in-law) was an equally avid Hull Kingston Rovers fan, and arrived decked out in red and white. Mary Harrison, the County Secretary's wife, had to sit between them and keep the peace as Hull romped to a 29-12 victory to secure their third consecutive Yorkshire Cup.

DID YOU KNOW?

On the morning of the 1984/85 Yorkshire Cup Final (previous entry) ground staff at Boothferry Park discovered that pranksters had broken into the ground overnight and left on the pitch a team of gnomes painted in black and white – and, facing them, a solitary gnome in red and white with its head snapped off.

LAST

ENGLAND DEBUTANT CAPTAIN

NIGEL MELVILLE: ENGLAND 3 AUSTRALIA 19 AT TWICKENHAM STADIUM, WHITTON ROAD, TWICKENHAM, MIDDLESEX TW2 7BA ENGLAND. SATURDAY 3 NOVEMBER 1984.

Wasps scrum half Melville became the last player to make his debut as captain when he led England against the Wallabies. However, his career was limited to 13 international caps by a series of serious injuries which eventually forced his retirement at 27.

FIRST

TEST APPEARANCE BY ROB ANDREW

ENGLAND 22 ROMANIA 15 AT TWICKENHAM STADIUM, WHITTON ROAD, TWICKENHAM, MIDDLESEX TW2 7BA ENGLAND. SATURDAY 5 JANUARY 1985.

Rob Andrew began his club career with Nottingham where he spent a season before signing for Wasps. He made his Test debut against Romania and scored four penalties and two drop goals. He was a regular at fly-half for around ten years. His playing career was ended in 1999 after an injury in training.

LAST

CHALLENGE CUP FINAL ATTENDED BY A ROYAL

ONLY

RUGBY LEAGUE CHALLENGE CUP FINAL RESULT PREDICTED IN A WEST END PLAY

CASTLEFORD 15 HULL KINGSTON ROVERS 14 AT WEMBLEY STADIUM, EMPIRE WAY, MIDDLESEX HA9 0WS ENGLAND. 3PM SATURDAY 3 MAY 1986.

John Godber, the artistic director of Hull Truck Theatre Company, is the world's third most performed playwright, after Shakespeare and Alan Ayckbourn. His 1984 Comedy of the Year *Up'n'Under* tells the story of how ex-Wakefield Trinity hooker Arthur Hoyle makes the ludicrous bet that his lowly sevens team from the Wheatsheaf Arms in Hull can beat the mighty Cobblers Arms of Castleford – a team described in the mock-Shakespearian opening monologue as: "unbeaten gods of amateur rugby sevens, unbeaten many seasons with greatness thrust upon them".

In order for the villainous Reg Welsh to exact maximum humiliation on Arthur he arranges for the Wheatsheaf to have a bye to the final of the next sevens competition, where they inevitably meet the Cobblers. Arthur's references to *Rocky* remind the audience that the underdogs can win, and by a combination of luck and skill the Wheatsheaf make it to within one-point of victory with one minute to go. Forty seconds later they get a penalty and the chance of a famous one point victory. Arthur steps up to take the kick (Wakefield Trinity fans will understand the significance of his line: "I could kick this in my slippers"), strikes it beautifully, and both teams watch as the ball soars into the air, strikes the post... and bounces back towards Arthur. So the team from Hull loses to the team from Castleford by one point after missing the final kick of the game.

In the 1986 Challenge Cup Final, less than two years after the first performance of Godber's play, Castleford built up a seemingly unassailable 15-6 lead but Hull Kingston Rovers scored on sixty-seven minutes to make it 15-10. Then, in the last minute, they scored again to make it fifteen-15-14. John Dorahy stepped up to take a difficult but kickable conversion and, after an agonisingly long preparation, struck the ball beautifully. Both teams and 82,134 spectators watched the ball soar into the air... and drift to the left of the posts, leaving Castleford with the narrowest of victories and their fourth Challenge Cup. The cup was presented to Castleford captain John Joyner by HRH the Princess Alexandra: it was her third visit to the Challenge Cup Final, and the last to date by any member of the royal family.

DID YOU KNOW?

Not only did John Godber manage an uncanny prediction, he also helped inspire the result. *Up'n'Under* was on in the West End at the time of the 1986 final, and Castleford coach Malcolm Reilly made watching the play a part of his squad's match preparations. Castleford's Lance Todd Trophy winner Bob Beardmore (who scored the thirty-second minute drop-goal that made the one-point difference) recorded in his Wembley diary for Thursday 1 May: "After evening dinner we went to see a play called *Up and Under* [sic] at the Drury Lane Theatre in London. Most lads enjoyed it, especially Keith England on the front row!" Note: *Up'n'Under* was actually on at the Fortune Theatre, having opened there on 26 March 1985.

LAST

TEST APPEARANCE BY TONY WARD

IRELAND 32 TONGA 9 AT BALLYMORE STADIUM, CLYDE ROAD, HERSTON, QUEENSLAND, AUSTRALIA. 3PM WEDNESDAY 3 JUNE 1987.

Irish rugby's first poster boy Tony Ward was as well known for his looks as his ability on the pitch. Ward won nineteen caps for Ireland between 1978 and 1987, making his debut against Scotland at Lansdowne Road on 21 January 1978. In the Five Nations Championship he scored thirty-eight points, a record for a newcomer. During his career as an Ireland international he scored 113 points, including 29 penalties, seven conversions and four drop goals.

He was the first winner of a European Rugby Player Of The Year award for his performances in the 1979 Five Nations tournament. His last Test match was in a 32-9 win over Tonga during the 1987 Rugby World Cup. Ward also played football for both Shamrock Rovers and Limerick United.

FIRST
RUGBY LEAGUE CHALLENGE CUP
FINAL TO RAISE £1MILLION RECEIPTS

Halifax 19 St Helens 18 at Wembley Stadium, Empire Way,
Middlesex HA9 0WS England. 3pm Saturday 2 May 1987.

Halifax upset Saints to win the cup for the fifth time in their history with
a million pounds taken at the gate. It was the first win for Halifax since
1939 and the last before Wigan's great run of success.

FIRST
RED CARD SHOWN AT RUGBY UNION
WORLD CUP FINAL

**Huw Richards: Wales 6 New Zealand 49 at Ballymore
Stadium, 91 Clyde Road, Herston, Queensland 4006
Australia. 3pm Sunday 14 June 1987.**

Huw Richards was a lock for Neath when he was selected for Wales in
the first World Cup. In the group stages, he played against Tonga and
then came on as a replacement for Bob Norster against England in the
quarter-finals. He kept his place for the semis against the All Blacks. The
New Zealanders outplayed the Welsh side and tempers began to fray.
Coming out of a loose scrum, Richards thumped lock Gary Whetton
and then found himself punched unconscious by Kiwi number eight
Wayne "Buck" Shelford. When he came round Richards was shown
the red card by referee Kerry Fitzgerald. Richards was banned for one
week, which meant he missed the final match of the competition – the
third-place play-off against the Wallabies, which Wales won by a single
point – 22-21.

FIRST
RUGBY UNION WORLD CUP FINAL

NEW ZEALAND 29 FRANCE 9 AT EDEN PARK, REIMERS AVENUE,
KINGSLAND, AUCKLAND 1024 NEW ZEALAND. SATURDAY 20 JUNE 1987.

On 21 March 1985, the International Rugby Board voted to inaugurate
a rugby union World Cup: Australia, France and New Zealand voted
in favour but the Home Nations voted against, on the basis that it
would threaten the amateur status of the game (something that would
be officially swept away within ten years). Then South Africa voted
in favour causing a stalemate of four votes for each proposition. First
England capitulated, then Wales and the World Cup was born six to
two, only Ireland and Scotland voting against. Still nursing a grudge
ninety years after the schism (see 1895), the International Rugby Board
ignored the fact that rugby league had initiated a world cup thirty-one
years earlier (see 1954) and called the competition the Rugby World Cup,
choosing 1987 as the inaugural year to avoid a clash with the Olympics
or the World Cup (although it was the year of the fourth cricket World
Cup). The "Rugby World Cup" is now the world's third biggest sporting
tournament after those two long-established events. **The first rugby
union World Cup match** took place between New Zealand and Italy
before a disappointing crowd on Friday 22 May 1987 at Eden Park. Bob
Fordham of Australia was **the first referee to take charge of a World
Cup match**. The hosts won 70-6 and went on to win the inaugural final
at the same venue before a crowd of 48,035. All Blacks skipper John Kirk
became **the first captain to lift the new cup**.

DID YOU KNOW?

The first match of every rugby union World Cup has been started
using the same whistle, which bears an inscription stating that it
was used in the 1905 New Zealand versus England Test (which
the All Blacks won 15-0). The whistle is also thought to have
been used for the final of the 1924 Olympics, the last time rugby
featured in the Games (see 1924), and is known to have been used
in the 1925 New Zealand versus England Test at Twickenham, in
which Cyril Brownlie became the first rugby union player sent off
in an international.

LAST

RUGBY LEAGUE SYDNEY GRAND FINAL
AT THE SYDNEY CRICKET GROUND

MANLY-WARRINGAH 18 CANBERRA RAIDERS 8 AT
SYDNEY CRICKET GROUND, MOORE PARK, MOORE PARK
ROAD, SYDNEY, NEW SOUTH WALES 2021 AUSTRALIA.
SUNDAY 27 SEPTEMBER 1987.

Fifty thousand, two hundred and one spectators turned up to watch the last game at the SCG. Manly became the first team other than Canterbury-Bankstown or Parramatta to win the Grand Final during the 1980s. Ecstatic after the victory in the blistering heat, captain Paul "Fatty" Vautin declared: "I think I might be the first Queenslander to have captained a Sydney Premiership side." He was wrong – Arthur Beetson was the first, captaining Easts to Premiership victory in 1974 and 1975 – but he was the last player from any state to captain a side to victory at the Sydney Cricket Ground. It was an emotional farewell to a ground that had captured the imagination of fans and players alike. Johnny Raper said: "The Grand Final at the SCG is what every player in the Sydney competition stives for… it's sacrilege to play elsewhere," a sentiment echoed by Reg Gasnier: "There is something emotional about playing here. This is one of the great grounds of the world. Right up there with Wembley, Headingley and Cardiff Arms Park. It just doesn't seem right playing the Grand Final anywhere else."

FIRST

NATIONAL SPORTING HALL OF FAME
IN THE UK (RUGBY LEAGUE)

RUGBY LEAGUE HALL OF FAME, NATIONAL MUSEUM OF RUGBY
LEAGUE, GEORGE HOTEL, ST GEORGE'S SQUARE, HUDDERSFIELD
WEST YORKSHIRE HD1 1JA, ENGLAND. 1988.

The Rugby League Hall of Fame was inaugurated in 1988 with nine inaugural inductees: Harold Wagstaff (see 1914), Billy Batten, Albert Rosenfeld, Jonty Parkin, Jim Sullivan (see 1929 and 1934), Gus Risman,

Brian Bevan, Billy Boston (see 1954) and Alex Murphy (see 1974). In 1995, the centenary of the rugby league, the Royal Mail issued special commemorative stamps featuring five of the original Hall of Famers: Billy Batten, Brian Bevan, Jim Sullivan, Gus Risman and Harold Wagstaff. The Australian Rugby League Hall of Fame was established in 2002 with six inaugural inductees: Clive Churchill, Reg Gasnier (see 1987), Johnny Raper (see 1987), Graeme Langlands, Bob Fulton and Wally Lewis.

FIRST
OCCASION *SWING LOW SWEET CHARIOT*
WAS SUNG AT AN ENGLAND GAME

ENGLAND 35 IRELAND 3 AT TWICKENHAM STADIUM, WHITTON ROAD, TWICKENHAM, MIDDLESEX TW2 7BA ENGLAND. SATURDAY 19 MARCH 1988.

It was half-time in the Five Nations match and Ireland were winning 3-0 at Billy Williams's Cabbage Patch and the disconsolate but unbowed England team trudged back onto the pitch. As England began a fightback in which they scored thirty-five points without reply, the crowd broke into the negro spiritual *Swing Low Sweet Chariot* and the song has been associated with English rugby ever since.

FIRST
ENGLAND TEST MATCH
ON A SUNDAY

Australia 22 England 16 at Ballymore Stadium, 91 Clyde Road, Herston, Queensland 4006 Australia. Sunday 29 May 1988.

The first time England played on the Sabbath was Down Under against the Wallabies. It was not a great success and the second Test in the series was also played on a Sunday and England again lost, this time twenty-28-8. **The first Five Nations match played on a Sunday** was not held until 22 March 1998 when England beat Scotland 34-20 at Murrayfield.

FIRST

PLAYER CAPPED FOR IRELAND
AFTER REPRESENTING ANOTHER COUNTRY

BRIAN SMITH: IRELAND 6 NEW ZEALAND 23 AT LANSDOWNE ROAD, BALLSBRIDGE, DUBLIN 4 REPUBLIC OF IRELAND. SATURDAY 18 NOVEMBER 1989.

Born at St George, Queensland, Smith made six appearances for Australia in 1987 beginning against Korea on 17 May at Brisbane and ending against Argentina at Buenos Aires on 31 October. He scored a try against Ireland when he came on as a substitute in the World Cup as the Wallabies ran out 33-15 winners. Two years later, he began a Test career for Ireland and played for them nine times.

FIRST

OCCASION *FLOWER OF SCOTLAND*
WAS PLAYED AS SCOTLAND'S RUGBY ANTHEM
Scotland 13 England 7 at Murrayfield, Edinburgh EH12 5PJ Scotland. Saturday 17 March 1990.

In 1974, the British Lions toured South Africa and a continent of Scottish supporters belted out *Flower Of Scotland*. Billy Steele, the winger, encouraged his team-mates to join in the singing. It would be sixteen years, however, before the song, written in 1965 by Roy Williamson (1936-90) of the folk group The Corries, was officially adopted by Scotland. The song is about the victory of the Scots, led by Robert the Bruce, over King Edward II at the Battle of Bannockburn on 24 June 1314. It was adopted after unruly Scots drowned out *God Save The Queen* with incessant booing and jeering. Williamson died aged 54 of a brain tumour five months after the first rendition. The match at which it was played was the last in that year's competition for England and Scotland and up to that time both had won every match and one was on course for a Grand Slam. England had easily won their matches while Scotland had struggled in their games. It was a time of anti-Englishness: the Community Charge had been introduced badly in Scotland and many of the Scottish and English players had a genuine dislike of each other. England's Will Carling and Brian Moore were hate figures north of the border. On the day of the match, Scottish captain David Sole led out his team slowly and Gavin Hastings believes that action gave the Scots a psychological advantage.

Flower Of Scotland was sung with great gusto and then Scotland set off at a cracking pace, not allowing England to settle and forcing the Sassenachs to make errors. Craig Chalmers struck two penalties before Jeremy Guscott scored a magisterial try for the visitors, England's first at Murrayfield for ten years. Chalmers hit another penalty to make it 9-4 at half-time. Play became even more frantic in the second half but Tony Stanger scored a try and despite a penalty from Rob Andrew, it was Scotland's day and they finished champions (fourteenth time), winners of the Grand Slam (third time), Calcutta Cup and the Centenary Quaich.

FIRST

ENGLAND RUGBY UNION
PLAYER TO WIN 50 CAPS

RORY UNDERWOOD: ENGLAND 15 AUSTRALIA 40 AT SYDNEY FOOTBALL STADIUM, DRIVER AVENUE, MOORE PARK, NEW SOUTH WALES 2021 AUSTRALIA. 3PM SATURDAY 27 JULY 1991.

The winger made his first appearance for England against Ireland at Twickenham on 18 February 1984 in the Five Nations match that the home side won by 12-9. It was in the semi-final of the World Cup that Underwood gained his fiftieth cap. After the game, Underwood was given the ball as a souvenir causing David Campese, the Australian winger, to joke that "it was the only time he got the ball in the game". In all Underwood won eighty-five caps for England and a further six for the British Lions. His last match for England was also against Ireland at Twickenham on 16 March 1996 and, in an almost perfect synchronicity, England won although this time the margin was slightly greater – 28-15.

LAST
MINER TO PLAY FOR WALES (RUGBY UNION)

GARIN JENKINS: WALES 3 FRANCE 36 AT PARC DES PRINCES, 24 RUE DU COMMANDANT GUILBAUD, 75016 PARIS, FRANCE. SATURDAY 2 MARCH 1991.

Born at Ynysybwl, Garin Jenkins is the (to date) 126th and last miner to play rugby for Wales. He was the most capped Welsh hooker with fifty-eight caps until Matthew Rees overtook his record on 14 June 2014.

LAST
ABANDONED RUGBY TEST (RUGBY UNION)

USA EAGLES 3 FRANCE 10 AT OBSERVATORY PARK, COLORADO SPRINGS, COLORADO, UNITED STATES OF AMERICA. SATURDAY 20 JULY 1991.

In the summer of 1991, France travelled to America to play four matches in the warm-up to the World Cup including two Tests against USA Eagles. The second of the matches began in a storm and the weather got worse. The stadium was nearly hit by lightning (some reports state that the scoreboard was, indeed, struck by lightning) and the referee Albert Adams called the game off after forty-two minutes with Les Bleus leading 10-3. France captain Serge Blanco had scored the thirty-eighth and last Test try of his career.

LAST
WINNERS OF RUGBY LEAGUE COUNTY CUPS

YORKSHIRE: WAKEFIELD TRINITY 29 SHEFFIELD EAGLES 16 AT ELLAND ROAD, LEEDS, WEST YORKSHIRE LS11 0ES ENGLAND. SUNDAY 18 OCTOBER 1992.

LANCASHIRE: WIGAN 5 ST HELENS 4 AT KNOWSLEY ROAD, ECCLESTON, ST HELENS, MERSEYSIDE, ENGLAND. SUNDAY 18 OCTOBER 1992.

One of the traditions abandoned in the change of structure from the Rugby League Championship to Super League was that of the County Cups and the county organisations behind them.

The last county cup finals were played in 1993/94 with Wakefield Trinity the last winners of the Yorkshire Cup and Wigan completing the circle as the last winners of the Lancashire Cup, having been the first winners in 1905.

FIRST
ENGLAND "BLOOD BIN" REPLACEMENT

Dewi Morris: England 24 Scotland 12 at Twickenham Stadium, Whitton Road, Twickenham, Middlesex TW2 7BA England. 3.05pm Saturday 18 March 1995.

In 1993, temporary replacements were allowed where a player had spilled blood. In 1995 in a match where the Grand Slam, Triple Crown and the Calcutta Cup were all at stake scrum half Dewi Morris came on in the 16th minute for Kyran Bracken. In the 22nd minute Bracken was fit enough to return to the action. England went on to triumph in the match.

FIRST
RUGBY LEAGUE
SUPER LEAGUE
SATURDAY 8 APRIL 1995.

On 8 April 1995, Maurice Lindsay, the CEO of the Rugby Football League, announced that the owners of BSkyB were offering £87m over five years for a super league of fourteen rugby league teams competing in the summer. The **first match took place on 29 March 1996** at Charletty Stadium in Paris and Paris St Germain beat Sheffield Eagles 30-24.

FIRST
MAJOR SPORTING EVENT TO TAKE PLACE IN AFRICA

FIRST
TIME RUGBY UNION WORLD CUP HELD IN ONE COUNTRY

LAST
RUGBY UNION WORLD CUP IN AMATEUR ERA

Rugby Union World Cup. South Africa. Thursday 25 May-Saturday 24 June 1995.

The 1995 Rugby World Cup was the third iteration, the first World Cup in which every match was held in the same country and the first major sporting event held in Africa. South Africa played host three years after its re-admittance to international rugby and won the competition. In August 1995, the International Rugby Football Board opened the sport to professionalism.

FIRST
FOREIGN RUGBY UNION COACH APPOINTED BY IRELAND

MURRAY KIDD: IRISH RUGBY FOOTBALL UNION, 10/12 LANSDOWNE ROAD, DUBLIN 4 REPUBLIC OF IRELAND. FRIDAY 13 OCTOBER 1995.

Murray Kidd was born at Te Kuiti, New Zealand in 1953 and while a 17-year-old schoolboy was picked for Taranaki against the 1971 British Lions. In 1995, he was appointed Ireland's first foreign-born coach and before he resigned in January 1997, he oversaw three victories and six defeats. Another foreigner, Brian Ashton from England, replaced him.

ONLY

CLUB TO WIN THE
RUGBY LEAGUE CHALLENGE CUP
EIGHT TIMES IN SUCCESSION

ONLY

CLUB TO WIN THE
RUGBY LEAGUE CHAMPIONSHIP
SEVEN TIMES IN SUCCESSION

ONLY

CLUB TO DO THE DOUBLE
SIX TIMES IN SUCCESSION
WIGAN WARRIORS. ENGLAND. 1996.

Their rivals may be reluctant to admit it but Wigan are by far the most successful club in the history of British rugby league and, though they may not have matched St George's eleven Sydney Premierships in a row (see 1966), their combination of league and cup success arguably makes them the most successful in the world. The club, founded in 1872 as Wigan Wasps, was a founder member of the Northern Rugby Football Union (see 1895) and has dominated the game ever since, but never more so than from 1988 to 1996, when they won eight consecutive Challenge Cup finals, seven consecutive championship titles and six consecutive league and cup doubles. Challenge Cup domination began in 1988 with a comprehensive 32-12 demolition of holders Halifax and continued with victories over St Helens in 1989 and Warrington in 1990 (making them the only club to win the cup three times in succession), then St Helens again, Castleford, Widnes, and Leeds twice in succession in 1994 and 1995, finally losing to Salford in the fifth round of the 1995/96 cup (Salford lost to St Helens, the eventual winners, in the next round). In 1989/90, Wigan managed a league and cup double, and didn't relinquish the league title until after winning the Centenary Championship of 1995/96 – a record seven consecutive titles, which overlapped with six of their Challenge Cup successes. In the meantime they also became the first club to win the World Club Challenge three times (in 1987, 1991 and 1994), the only British club to win the World Club Challenge in Australia, the first rugby league club named BBC Sports Team Of The Year and the first rugby league club to win the Middlesex Sevens (see overleaf).

FIRST
RUGBY UNION V RUGBY LEAGUE MATCH
UNDER RUGBY LEAGUE RULES

FIRST
PLAYER TO SCORE A RUGBY LEAGUE
TRY FOR A RUGBY UNION TEAM

WIGAN 82 BATH 6 AT MAINE ROAD, MOSS SIDE, MANCHESTER M14 7WN ENGLAND. WEDNESDAY 8 MAY 1996.

As a rugby league match Wigan v Bath was no contest but as an historic occasion it was unprecedented – the first first-class cross-code match played under rugby league rules since the "great divide" of 1895, one hundred and one years earlier. (Two cross-code matches were played under union rules during the Second World War; see 1943). The spur for this change in attitude was that the previous year the Rugby Football Union had bowed to the inevitable and openly accepted professionalism, after which Wigan and Bath, the champions of each code, arranged two exhibition matches, one under each set of rules. First came the rugby league match at Maine Road. As expected, Wigan comprehensively demolished Bath, but the scale of the victory surprised many people – particularly as Wigan withdrew Henry Paul and Andy Farrell after only twenty minutes, played Tuigamala for less than half the game, and at half-time agreed to a request from Bath to relax the rules to allow unlimited substitutions. Jon Callard became **the first rugby union player to score a rugby league try for a rugby union team**, converting his own try for Bath's only points. Bath salvaged some pride for club and code in the return match under rugby union rules at Twickenham on 25 May, which they won by 44-19.

FIRST

RUGBY LEAGUE PLAYER TO
SCORE A HAT-TRICK AT WEMBLEY

ROBBIE PAUL: BRADFORD BULLS 32 ST HELENS 40 AT WEMBLEY STADIUM, EMPIRE WAY, MIDDLESEX HA9 0WS ENGLAND. 2.30PM SATURDAY 27 APRIL 1996.

The first Challenge Cup of the Super League era was a points bonanza – the highest score by a winning team, the highest score by a losing team and, by definition, the highest aggregate score. A total of seventy-two points were scored, with nine different players scoring a total of thirteen tries – three of them from Bradford's Robbie Paul, who thus managed a coveted Wembley first, and the Lance Todd Trophy, despite being on the losing side. (See 1902.)

FIRST

RUGBY LEAGUE CLUB
TO PLAY AT TWICKENHAM

FIRST

RUGBY LEAGUE CLUB
TO WIN THE RUGBY UNION
MIDDLESEX SEVENS

Wigan. Twickenham Stadium, Whitton Road, Twickenham, Middlesex TW2 7BA England. 12.40pm Saturday 11 May 1996.

Twickenham has been the traditional home of rugby union so it was some years before a team from the northern code played a match there. Wigan played for charity and at the request of the Rugby Football Union with Jason Robinson, Va'aiga Tuigamala, Martin Offiah and Shaun Edwards in their side.

FIRST

SUPER LEAGUE CHAMPIONS

FIRST

SEASON OF SUMMER RUGBY LEAGUE

ST HELENS. 1996.

The first season of Super League began on 29 March 1996, following the Rugby Football League's decision to switch to playing in summer and the signing of a lucrative contract with BSkyB. Each team plays twenty-three games between February and July: eleven at home and eleven away plus a "Magic Weekend" game at a neutral venue.

St Helens won the inaugural Super League title by one point from Wigan (forty points to thirty-nine).

FIRST

ENGLAND TACTICAL REPLACEMENT

FIRST

TIME ENGLAND
HAD A SPONSOR'S NAME ON SHIRT

England 54 Italy 21 at Twickenham Stadium, Whitton Road, Twickenham, Middlesex TW2 7BA England. 3pm Saturday 23 November 1996.

On 4 November 1996, the International Rugby Board amended its laws to allow replacements for tactical reasons and in their next Test Rob Hardwick made his only appearance for England, coming on as a replacement for Jason Leonard in the drubbing of Italy in the Five Nations tournament. England had seven debutants in the match attended by 45,000 fans when they bore a sponsor's name – Cellnet – for the first time on their shirts.

FIRST

YELLOW CARD (SIN BIN)
SHOWN AT INTERNATIONAL RUGBY UNION

JAMES HOLBECK: AUSTRALIA 22 SOUTH
AFRICA 61 AT LOFTUS VERSFELD STADIUM,
KIRKNESS STREET, PRETORIA 0007 SOUTH
AFRICA. 5PM 23 AUGUST 1997.

The yellow and red cards to signify bookings and sendings off were
invented by former football referee Ken Aston. In 1962 he had been the
referee during the match between Chile and Italy and needed an armed
guard to get off the pitch.

Four years later, he watched in dismay as the Argentineans surrounded
the West German referee Rudolf Kreitlein after he sent off their captain
Antonio Rattín for "violence of the tongue" even though neither man
could understand the other.

The next day, Aston found that the Charlton brothers had both been
booked but neither knew. As he drove his MG home from his office
one day, he got his eureka moment when he was caught at traffic lights.
FIFA introduced the red and yellow cards in time for the 1970 World
Cup. In the opening match Soviet defender Evgeny Lochev became the
first player shown a yellow card.

Four other players followed him into the referee's notebook but not
one red card was shown at the tournament. Rugby was much slower in
introducing the innovation.

The first was shown to England's Ben Clarke for stamping on Simon
Geoghegan, his Bath club-mate, during the 1995 Ireland-England Five
Nations match in Dublin. However, in those days a yellow card was
merely a warning.

The first yellow card recipient to go to the sin bin was James Holbeck
of Australia against South Africa. The card was still just cautionary,
which is why Joost van der Westhuizen and Pieter du Randt did not
leave the field. Holbeck returned to the game with a minute left on the
clock.

FIRST
SUPER LEAGUE GRAND FINAL WINNERS

WIGAN WARRIORS 10 LEEDS RHINOS 4 AT OLD TRAFFORD, SIR MATT BUSBY WAY, OLD TRAFFORD, MANCHESTER M16 0RA ENGLAND. SATURDAY 24 OCTOBER 1998.

For the first two years of Super League (see 1996) the champions were decided under the traditional system of who finished at the top of the table, but in 1998 Super League adopted the Australian system of a series of play-offs between the top five (later six) clubs. That year Wigan Warriors finished four points clear of Leeds Rhinos at the top of the table (and with a points difference of 540), and beat Leeds in the first Grand Final to claim the Super League title.

ONLY
INTERNATIONAL RUGBY UNION
TRY SCORED IN LESS THAN 10 SECONDS

JOHN LESLIE: SCOTLAND 33 WALES 20 AT MURRAYFIELD, EDINBURGH EH12 5PJ SCOTLAND. SATURDAY 6 FEBRUARY 1999.

Remarkably, Leo Price managed to score a try in exactly ten seconds for England against Wales at Twickenham on 20 January 1923. Even more remarkably, Scotland managed an even faster one in 1999. Duncan Hodge feigned to kick off to the right for Scotland and the Welsh defence organised itself accordingly: then, as he took his run up, Hodge switched direction and kicked to the left. Scotland's John Leslie, in hot pursuit of the ball, snatched it from the grasp of the Welsh catcher and sprinted over the line while most of the Welsh defence was still adjusting to the change of direction of the kick-off. Several action replays established that Leslie had scored in just nine seconds.

LAST

FIVE NATIONS MATCH

WALES 32 ENGLAND 31 AT WEMBLEY STADIUM, EMPIRE WAY, MIDDLESEX HA9 0WS ENGLAND. 4PM SATURDAY 11 APRIL 1999.

The last Five Nations was played at Wembley as a home match for Wales while the Millennium Stadium was being built. England had to win the match to be victorious in the competition but fell at the final hurdle handing the title to Scotland on points difference. With the addition of Italy in 2000, the competition became the Six Nations and the first winners were England.

FIRST

TIME ENGLAND DID NOT WEAR WHITE SHIRTS

ONLY

TIME ENGLAND DID NOT WEAR WHITE SHORTS

England 15 Australia 22 at Stadium Australia, Edwin Flack Avenue, Sydney Olympic Park, Sydney, New South Wales 2127 Australia. Saturday 26 June 1999.

It is not known why England play in white although it is likely because Rugby School also play in that colour. England have played in white in all but two matches. For the Test match against Australia to celebrate that country's centenary they wore blue shirts with thin red and white hoops.

LAST
RUGBY LEAGUE CHALLENGE CUP FINAL
AT THE EMPIRE STADIUM, WEMBLEY

**LEEDS RHINOS 52 LONDON BRONCOS 16 AT WEMBLEY
STADIUM, EMPIRE WAY, MIDDLESEX HA9 0WS ENGLAND.
SATURDAY 1 MAY 1999.**

The 1999 Challenge Cup was the last year the Challenge Cup Final was played there before the stadium closed for redevelopment. Leeds Rhinos picked up their first major silverware since 1978. The Lance Todd Trophy went to Leroy Rivett, who had become **the first player to score four tries in a Challenge Cup Final**.

ONLY
BROTHERS TO PLAY AGAINST
EACH OTHER IN A RUGBY UNION
WORLD CUP MATCH

**Steve and Graeme Bachop: Samoa 43 Japan 9 at Racecourse Ground,
Mold Road, Wrexham, Wales. 1pm Sunday 3 October 1999.**

A rugby union player can qualify to play for a nation through birth, parentage, grandparentage or residence, something which has led to two pairs of New Zealand-born brothers facing each other at Test level: Tana Umaga for New Zealand against Mike Umaga for Samoa in June 1999, and Pita Alatini for New Zealand against Sam Alatini for Tonga in June 2000. Until the rules were changed on 1 January 2000, players could also play for more than one nation, which led to the unique situation of one pair of brothers – Graeme and Steve Bachop – playing together for New Zealand in four Tests (at scrum half and fly half respectively in 1994) and later facing each other while representing two other nations in a World Cup match. By the time of the 1999 World Cup, scrum half Graeme had qualified through residence to play for Japan, and in their opening match he found himself playing against Steve, who was by then playing fly half for Samoa. It is the only time two brothers have played against each other in a World Cup match.

LAST

RUGBY UNION
TEST MATCH AT ATHLETIC PARK

NEW ZEALAND 54 FRANCE 7 AT ATHLETIC PARK, NEWTOWN, WELLINGTON, NEW ZEALAND. SATURDAY 26 JUNE 1999.

The spiritual home of New Zealand rugby opened on 6 April 1896. It also played host from 1923 to the country's leading football tournament, the Chatham Cup. The stadium was often beset by strong winds that made the Millard Stand sway much to the consternation of spectators in their seats. The 1961 All Black Test match versus France was played in hurricane force winds. After much consideration it was decided not to revamp the stadium but to demolish it. The last Test match was against France and the last rugby match was four months later on 10 October 1999, between Wellington and Otago NPC teams, with Wellington running out the victors 36-16. A village for old aged pensioners now stands on the site.

ONLY

SIX NATIONS SIDE TO BEAT
SCOTLAND ON FIRST MEETING

ITALY 34 SCOTLAND 20 AT STADIO FLAMINIO, VIALE DELLO STADIO FLAMINIO, I-00196 ROME 5 ITALY. SATURDAY 5 FEBRUARY 2000.

Scotland triumphed against all of the Six Nations on their first meeting – she beat England at Raeburn Place in 1871 (see 1871); Ireland 4-0 at Ormeau, Belfast on 19 February 1877; Wales by three goals to one at Raeburn Place on 8 January 1883, France 27-0 at Inverleith in January 1910 – until they clashed with the Azzurri on the opening day of the 2000 Six Nations. Before the game, Italy had been rated as 250-1 shots to win the Six Nations in their first season. It would be the Italians' only victory in the competition as they won the wooden spoon.

FIRST

IRISH PLAYER
SENT TO THE SIN BIN

**PADDY JOHNS: IRELAND 27 FRANCE 25 AT STADE DE FRANCE,
93216 SAINT-DENIS FRANCE. SATURDAY 19 MARCH 2000.**

Ulster second-row Johns was only on the pitch for a few minutes before
he was shown a yellow card by Paul Honiss, the referee, for killing the
ball. Johns was dropped from the squad for his indiscretion.

LAST

RUGBY MATCH TO ATTRACT
MORE THAN 100,000 SPECTATORS (RUGBY UNION)
Australia 35 New Zealand 39: Bledisloe Cup at Stadium Australia,
Edwin Flack Avenue, Sydney Olympic Park, Sydney, New South
Wales 2127 Australia. Saturday 15 July 2000.

For forty-five years the official record crowd for a rugby match of either
code was 102,569 at the 1954 rugby league Challenge Cup Final replay
(see 1954). Then the massive Stadium Australia opened in the Sydney
Olympic Park, with an official capacity of 110,000. The first sporting
event held there was a rugby league first round double-header on 6 March
1999, when 104,583 watched Newcastle play Manly and Parramatta
play St George-Illawarra to set a new world record crowd for a rugby
match. This record was then broken by the 1999 rugby union Bledisloe
Cup match between Australia and New Zealand (107,042) and the 1999
rugby league Grand Final between Melbourne Storm and St George-
Illawarra (107,999). The last rugby match of either code to attract a
crowd of over 100,000 will probably remain so for some time to come,
because in 2003 the stadium was reconfigured with a reduced capacity
of 83,500 for a rectangular field and 81,500 for an oval field. The match
in question was the 2000 Bledisloe Cup, when 109,874 witnessed what
many rugby union fans refer to as "The Greatest Ever Rugby Match".
The All Blacks stormed to a 24-0 lead after just eleven minutes but a
remarkable comeback from Australia made it 24-all at half-time. After
a close, tense second half Jonah Lomu scored for the All Blacks to seal a
memorable victory by just four points.

FIRST

RUGBY UNION PLAYER TO SCORE 1,000 INTERNATIONAL POINTS

NEIL JENKINS: WALES 43 FRANCE 35 AT STADE DE FRANCE, 93216 SAINT-DENIS FRANCE. SATURDAY 17 MARCH 2001.

Neil Jenkins made his first XV debut for Pontypridd on 14 April 1990. His first international appearance came nine months later on 19 January 1991 against England. It was in that game he scored the first points of his career – three thanks to a penalty. In the match against France he became the first rugby player to break the 1,000 international points mark, with a twenty-eight-point haul featuring a full house of a try, conversion, drop-goal, and penalty. His eighty-seventh and last Test was on 1 November 2002 in Wrexham against Romania and Wales ran out 40-3 winners. In his career, he scored 1,049 points (eleven tries, 130 conversions, 235 penalties and ten drop goals) and a further forty-one points (a solitary conversion and thirteen penalties) during his four caps for the British & Irish Lions for a total of 1,090 points. Jonny Wilkinson subsequently broke Jenkins's world record.

FIRST

RUGBY UNION CLUB TO
RETAIN THE HEINEKEN CUP

Leicester Tigers 15 Munster 9 at Millennium Stadium, Westgate Street, Cardiff CF10 1NS Wales. Saturday 25 May 2002.

In a pulsating final, Leicester Tigers became the first club to retain the Heineken Cup, but in Ireland the match is remembered not for the excitement but for the so-called "Hand of Back" incident in the tense closing stages of the game (a reference to Maradona's "Hand of God" in the World Cup). After two disallowed Leicester "tries" and two Munster penalties it was, ironically, an Irishman in the Leicester ranks – Geordan Murphy – who finally put points on the board for the Tigers, scoring an unconverted try to reduce Munster's half-time lead to 6-5. Ronan O'Gara put Munster 9-5 ahead with another penalty immediately after the break but then the arrival of the cavalry, in the form of Leicester substitute Harry Ellis, galvanised the Tigers into action and a converted Austin Healey try gave them the lead for the first time in the game. Tension built during the final quarter as the first-half roles were reversed: Leicester scored a penalty and Munster had a "try" disallowed. Then, at 15-9 down but still within reach of a win, Munster were awarded a scrum in front of the Leicester posts. Munster won the ball but before they could do anything with it Leicester's Neil Back appeared to knock the ball out of Peter Stringer's grasp. None of the officials spotted the infringement and Munster's last chance had gone – the Tigers held on to a controversial victory and an historic first.

ONLY

SON OF AN ENGLAND TEST CRICKETER AND FIRST-CLASS FOOTBALLER TO PLAY FIRST-CLASS CRICKET, RUGBY UNION, RUGBY LEAGUE

LIAM BOTHAM. ENGLAND. AUGUST 2003.

During his time off from being one of Scunthorpe United's most famous strikers, Ian Botham also made a name for himself as one of England's greatest cricketers.

Being an all-rounder obviously runs in the family – his son Liam played county cricket for Hampshire in 1996 (taking former England captain Mike Gatting's wicket on his county debut) and then, perhaps realising he had too much to live up to, gave up cricket in 1997 after three first class matches to play rugby union for West Hartlepool, Cardiff (1997-2000), Newcastle Falcons (2000-03) and England under-21s. In 2003, he switched to rugby league, signing for Leeds Rhinos (2003-05), Leeds Tykes (2003-04) and then Wigan Warriors (2005).

FIRST

YELLOW CARD SHOWN
AT RUGBY UNION
WORLD CUP FINAL

MANUEL CONTEPOMI: ARGENTINA 8 AUSTRALIA 24 AT STADIUM AUSTRALIA, EDWIN FLACK AVENUE, SYDNEY OLYMPIC PARK, SYDNEY, NEW SOUTH WALES 2127 AUSTRALIA. FRIDAY 10 OCTOBER 2003.

Yellow cards were introduced in the World Cup in 2003. The first was shown to Contepomi for an illegal tackle on Wallaby Mat Rogers in the opening match of the competition. The man who brandished the first yellow card was Paul Honiss of New Zealand.

FIRST

CLUB TO WIN THE
RUGBY LEAGUE CHALLENGE CUP AND
SUPER LEAGUE GRAND FINAL
IN THE SAME SEASON

FIRST
RUGBY LEAGUE CHALLENGE CUP FINAL
PLAYED IN WALES

BRADFORD BULLS 22 LEEDS RHINOS 20 AT MILLENNIUM STADIUM, WESTGATE STREET, CARDIFF CF10 1NS WALES. SATURDAY 26 APRIL 2003 AND BRADFORD BULLS 25 WIGAN WARRIORS 12 AT OLD TRAFFORD, SIR MATT BUSBY WAY, OLD TRAFFORD, MANCHESTER M16 0RA ENGLAND. SATURDAY 18 OCTOBER 2003.

In 2003, Bradford Bulls became the first club to win the Challenge Cup and Super League Grand Final in the same season. They beat off the challenge of Leeds Rhinos in front of 71,212 fans at the Millennium Stadium, Cardiff and then triumphed over Wigan Warriors in the Grand Final before a record, sell-out crowd of 65,537 at Manchester's Old Trafford.

FIRST

MAN TO PLAY IN THE
RUGBY UNION AND CRICKET
WORLD CUP FINALS TOURNAMENTS
IN THE SAME YEAR

RUDI VAN VUUREN: NAMIBIA 45 LOST TO AUSTRALIA 301 FOR 6 AT NORTH WEST CRICKET STADIUM, POTCHEFSTROOM 2520 SOUTH AFRICA. THURSDAY 27 FEBRUARY 2003; NAMIBIA 7 ROMANIA 37 AT YORK PARK, INVERMAY ROAD, LAUNCESTON, TASMANIA 7250 AUSTRALIA. THURSDAY 30 OCTOBER 2003.

As well as being a sporting all-rounder Van Vuuren, a white Namibian, is also a doctor and runs a wildlife sanctuary. A medium-pace bowler, he competed in the 2003 Cricket World Cup against Australia, and later the same year he played fly half against Romania in the Rugby World Cup finals. His own assessment of his cricketing skills is that he is "not that talented". As for his rugby, he says: "How can I compete with Jonny Wilkinson? He would not expect to walk into my surgery and treat my patients."

ONLY

REFEREE TO OFFICIATE
AT TWO RUGBY UNION
WORLD CUP FINALS

André Watson: Australia 35 France 12 at Millennium Stadium, Westgate Street, Cardiff CF10 1NS Wales. Saturday 6 November 1999. Australia 17 England 20 at Telstra Stadium, Edwin Flack Avenue, Sydney Olympic Park, Sydney, New South Wales 2127 Australia. Saturday 22 November 2003.

Born at Germiston, Transvaal, South Africa, André Jacobus Watson began officiating in 1987, becoming full time eight years later. He refereed 100 Currie Cup matches including seven cup finals and five

Super Rugby finals. His first international match as a referee was in 1996 between Australia and Canada. He took charge of the 1999 World Cup Final at Cardiff and then four years later blew the whistle at the match between England and the holders Australia. He retired in 2007.

ONLY
RUGBY PLAYER TO WIN BBC SPORTS PERSONALITY OF THE YEAR AWARD

JONNY WILKINSON BBC TELEVISION CENTRE, WOOD LANE, LONDON W12 ENGLAND. SUNDAY 14 DECEMBER 2003

First presented in 1954 (the winner then was Christopher Chataway, the athlete), the first rugby player to win the award was Jonny Wilkinson. The runner-up was Martin Johnson. In 1971, Barry John came third (behind HRH the Princess Anne and George Best) and three years later Willie John McBride also took the bronze medal. In 1991, Will Carling was runner-up to Liz McColgan. In 2013, Leigh Halfpenny was also runner-up (to Andy Murray).

ONLY
RUGBY UNION FAN TO CUT OFF HIS TESTICLES TO CELEBRATE A WIN

Geoff Huish, Senghenydd, Caerphilly, CF83 Wales. Wales 11 England 9 at Millennium Stadium, Westgate Street, Cardiff CF10 1NS Wales. Saturday 5 February 2005.

On 6 February 1993 at the National Stadium, Wales beat England 10-9 in the Five Nations Championship. It would be their last victory for a dozen years and some of their fans became a little concerned at the lack of success. Geoff Huish, 31, was one such supporter so he probably thought he was making a safe bet when he told his friend Gethin Probert,

"If Wales win, I'll cut my balls off." Huish listened to the game on the radio at home in Senghenydd and Wales won 11-9 with Gavin Henson clinching victory. Huish recalls, "After the match I got up for a pee and saw [a pair of wire] cutters in the bathroom. Gethin had left them after repairing the chain on my toilet. I remembered what I'd said and thought he had left them for me. I thought, "Oh no, I haven't got to do anything like that, have I?" Then I thought, "You can do it," so I started hacking away at my tackle. It took about ten minutes and there was quite a lot of pain but I just kept going. The cutters were blunt so I had to keep snipping. I cut my penis as well. There was a lot of blood but not as much as you would expect." Huish collected his testicles from the lavatory pan and went to Gethin Probert's house but his friend was out so he walked to the Leigh Social Club with his testicles in a plastic blue bag to prove he'd fulfilled his promise. He said, "The Leigh was packed with rugby fans. I went in and shouted out, 'I've done it'. I took my balls out and passed them in the bag to a friend. Some people then laid me on the floor." Friends called an ambulance and put his testicles in a pint glass of ice but doctors were unable to reattach them. Later, Huish said, "I think about what happened every day and still haven't come up with a good reason why. I'd had a lot going on and felt a bit down. I can't have kids now but still want a family – maybe I'll adopt."

<hr/>

FIRST
TRIPLE CROWN WINNERS
IRELAND. SATURDAY 18 MARCH 2006

Although the concept of the Triple Crown has been around since the start of the Home Nations Championship (indeed the term originated in England in the mid-19th century in horse racing), it was not until 2006 that a physical trophy was presented. Ireland were the first recipients of the sixteen and a half inches wide and two inches deep silver dish although France were victorious in the championship. Hamilton & Inches of Edinburgh and London designed the trophy.

FIRST

RUGBY LEAGUE CLUB
SPONSORED BY A FILM

ONLY

RUGBY LEAGUE CLUB
PART OWNED BY RUSSELL CROWE

SOUTH SYDNEY RABBITOHS. SUNDAY 19 MARCH 2006.

On this day New Zealand-born Hollywood actor and long-term Rabbitohs fan Russell Crowe and his business partner Peter Holmes à Court bought 75 per cent of the Rabbitohs (see 1929) for AUS$3m. In 2005, the Rabbitohs became the first rugby league club sponsored by a film, when Crowe promoted his film *Cinderella Man* on their jerseys.

DID YOU KNOW?

Crowe employs former Souths forward Mark Carroll as a bodyguard and personal trainer.

ONLY

RUGBY LEAGUE TEAM
RELEGATED FROM SUPER LEAGUE
WITHOUT FINISHING BOTTOM

CASTLEFORD. 2005/06.

At the end of the 2005/06 season, Castleford found themselves in a relegation battle away to Wakefield Trinity Wildcats at Belle Vue, a match that was called "The Battle of Belle Vue". Wakefield ran out winners condemning Castleford to relegation even though they finished second bottom. Castleford went down because the French side Catalans Dragons had been given immunity from relegation and Wigan Warriors who were guilty of breaching wages cap rules.

ONLY

PLAYER TO WIN THE

RUGBY LEAGUE LANCE TODD TROPHY

THREE TIMES

**SEAN LONG, ST HELENS 42 HUDDERSFIELD GIANTS 12,
TWICKENHAM STADIUM, WHITTON ROAD, TWICKENHAM,
MIDDLESEX TW2 7BA ENGLAND. SATURDAY 26 AUGUST 2006.**

Scrum half Sean "Longy" Long played for Wigan Warriors and Widnes Vikings before signing for St Helens in 1997 and becoming a vital part of Saints' phenomenal success since then. After winning the Lance Todd Trophy in St Helens' Challenge Cup victories over Bradford Bulls in 2001 and Wigan Warriors in 2004, he won it for an unprecedented third time in the 2006 victory over Huddersfield Giants.

ONLY

INTERNATIONAL RUGBY CAPTAIN

CONVICTED OF MURDER

(RUGBY UNION)

Marc Cécillon at Grenoble, France. Friday 10 November 2006.

Just before midnight on Saturday 7 August 2004, Marc Cécillon, the "Calm Man" of French rugby union, shot his wife, Chantal, at a party in front of sixty guests at Saint-Savin, Poitou-Charentes near Lyon. 6ft 4in Cécillon, who had turned to alcohol since retiring in 1995 from the national side he had captained five times, was five or six times over the drink-drive limit and claimed the next day to have no memory of what happened.

Cécillon arrived at the party, a barbecue in honour of his best friend Christian Beguy's birthday. He had spent the day drinking and playing petanque with his close friend and the former France captain Jean-

Francois Tordo. By 10pm he was abusively drunk so at 11pm when M Beguy's wife, Babeth, suggested Cécillon eat something to mop up the alcohol, he lost his temper and slapped her hard enough to cause a black eye. Cécillon insisted that Chantal leave with him but she refused so he went home and returned with his Taurus Brazil Magnum .357 revolver. He shot her five times in the head and chest. As soon as Cécillon had fired the gun, Alexandre, the Beguys' teenage son, threw a huge concrete breeze block at Cécillon's head, but it "just bounced off, as if it had made no impression".

It took seventeen men to subdue the former Number 8 and when the police arrived he was still struggling, tied to a chair with electrical cord and asking for his dead wife. There were mutterings of a mistress and a son born out of wedlock. These were confirmed by the illegitimate child himself who turned out to have inherited his father's talent for rugby – he was the Racing Metro and France international centre Alexandre Dumoulin. "He was a drunk. He drank, he screwed, and he always got away with it because he was Marc Cécillon," said Tordo's wife Pascal. "That's what twenty years of alcohol does to you – little by little it destroys you. Marc could not cope with his life. When you kill your wife, you are killing your life."

During his trial, which began on 6 November 2006, Cécillon admitted shooting Chantal: "I wanted my wife to come back with me. I wanted the two of us to leave together," he told the court. "Why did I shoot? It is a question I shall ask myself all my life. I didn't plan anything. I wish I could understand." He denied murder, saying that he was depressed and drunk at the time and did not intend to kill her but that excuse didn't wash with the jury, who found him guilty of murder rather than the lesser charge of involuntary manslaughter. Cécillon's 26-year-old daughter, Angelique, broke down and sobbed, "I don't think my father intended to kill my mother," before making an emotional plea for the jury to show clemency, telling them that she missed both her parents and that her father had already been punished enough. However, the five-woman, four-man jury ignored her plea, deciding that he should serve twenty years rather than the fifteen the prosecution had requested. The sentence was later reduced to fourteen years on appeal and Cécillon was released on parole in July 2011.

LAST

MATCH AT LANSDOWNE ROAD

**LEINSTER 20 ULSTER 12 AT LANSDOWNE ROAD,
BALLSBRIDGE, DUBLIN 4 REPUBLIC OF IRELAND.
SUNDAY 31 DECEMBER 2006**

On 26 November 2006, the stadium hosted its last international rugby match when Ireland beat the Pacific Islanders 61-17. Just over a month later, the same two teams that had competed in the first match played the last game before a crowd of 48,000 fans, a record attendance. The bulldozers moved in on 17 May 2007.

FIRST

RUGBY LEAGUE PLAYER TO COMPETE WITH AN OPPONENT'S TOOTH IN HIS HEAD

**Ben Czislowski: Wynnum Manly v Tweed Heads at
Kougari Oval, Wondall Road, Brisbane West, South
Australia, Australia. Sunday 1 April 2007.**

Prop Ben Czislowski made one appearance for Brisbane Broncos in 2004 and then played eight times for Canterbury Bulldogs in 2005 and 2006, both in the National Rugby League. He then dropped down and joined Wynnum. On April Fool's Day 2007 he collided with opposite number Matt Austin.

Wynnum's physio stitched up the wound and Czislowski played on. Some time later, he suffered an eye infection and complained of splitting headaches and lethargy. In the middle of July, he paid a visit to his GP and an examination revealed that he had a tooth embedded in his head.

FIRST

RUGBY LEAGUE CHALLENGE CUP FINAL
AT THE NEW WEMBLEY STADIUM

FIRST
CHALLENGE CUP FINAL
TO FEATURE A FOREIGN TEAM

FIRST
RUGBY LEAGUE PLAYER TO
SCORE A TRY AT THE NEW
WEMBLEY STADIUM

LAST
PAIR OF PLAYERS TO
SHARE THE LANCE TODD TROPHY

PAUL WELLENS AND LEON
PRYCE: ST HELENS 30 CATALANS
DRAGONS 8 AT WEMBLEY STADIUM,
MIDDLESEX HA9 0WS ENGLAND.
3.05PM SATURDAY 25 AUGUST 2007.

The 2007 Challenge Cup began in February 2007 and included teams from England, Wales, Scotland, France and Russia.

The preliminary round was dropped and teams from the National League were given byes to the third round while teams from the Super League entered in the fourth round. The final was played in stifling heat at Wembley.

ONLY
TEST WON BY PACIFIC ISLANDERS
LAST
TEST PLAYED BY PACIFIC ISLANDERS

PACIFIC ISLANDERS 25 ITALY 17 AT STADIO GIGLIO PIAZZALE ATLETI AZZURI D'ITALIA, 42122 REGGIO EMILIA RE, ITALY. SATURDAY 22 NOVEMBER 2008.

The Pacific Islands Rugby Alliance was formed in 2003 to take the financial burden off teams from that part of the world. The side was made up mainly of players from Fiji, Samoa and Tonga and played their first Test on 3 July 2004 against Australia at Adelaide Oval and they lost by 29-14. In fact, the Pacific Islanders lost every Test they played apart from the last when two tries from Vilimoni Deelesau and one from Kameli Ratuvou gave them a victory over the Azzurri.

The Pacific Islanders do not play in the World Cup as the individual nations compete under their own colours. Seru Rabeni and Moses Rauluni are **the only two players to have played in all nine Tests for the Pacific Islanders.** It seems that the Pacific Islanders will not play again as in July 2009 the Samoa Rugby Union left the group, claiming that it had not brought the expected financial benefits. Peter Schuster, the chairman of Samoa Rugby Union, said: "The original concept was basically to provide an opportunity [to play] every two years.

"There were two aims, to get revenue to help in the running of the activities of the unions [and] to provide players with the opportunity to play against tier one sides.

"But the International Rugby Board changed the schedule for the Pacific Islands team to play every four years. Every four years won't generate the revenue needed to run our rugby."

FIRST

RUGBY TEAM
TO PUT THEIR
TWITTER NAMES ON THEIR SHIRTS

LEEDS RHINOS 21 HULL 6 HEADINGLEY, LEEDS, WEST YORKSHIRE LS6 3BU ENGLAND. 8PM FRIDAY 6 JULY 2012.

Leeds Rhinos made rugby history when those players who had them took to the field with their Twitter handles rather than surnames on the back of their shirts. However, the Rugby Football League forbade Ryan Bailey from using his name @Hayemaker16 because they claimed it could be seen as inciting violence. Phil Daly, the club's media and PR manager, said: "We are always looking for ways to innovate and spread the word about Leeds Rhinos. With over 500 million users on Twitter worldwide it is massive around the globe and a tremendous vehicle for us to grow our brand." At the time of the match the Rhinos had more than 18,000 Twitter followers, a figure that has risen to almost 80,000. The Rhinos also wore a lime green and steel alternative shirt to help raise awareness and money for the Royal Navy & Royal Marine Charity as part of their third annual Armed Forces Day game. Twenty-one of the thirty-one members of the first-team squad were on Twitter.

The full list of players on Twitter is as follows:

Player/Twitter Name	Player/Twitter Name
Luke Ambler@Ambler09	Shaun Lunt@Shaun_Lunt
Ryan Bailey*@hayemaker16	Danny McGuire@DannyMcguire6
Luke Briscoe@lukebriscoee	Paul McShane@mcshane_paul
Rob Burrow@Rob7Burrow	Jamie Peacock@JamiePeacock10
Jamel Chisholm@jamelchisholm7	Brad Singleton@bradsingo
Chris Clarkson@chrisclarkson00	Daniel Smith@smithdaniel1
Brett Delaney@brettdelaney3	Lee Smith@Smith2Lee
Zak Hardaker@zakhardaker1	Jared Stewart@Jaredstewart9
Weller Hauraki@Weller_Hauraki	Stevie Ward@Ste_Ward
Liam Hood@Liamhood24	Kallum Watkins@kallum_watkins
Ian Kirke@IanKirke	Brent Webb@Brent_D_Webb79

* Bailey played with his surname on his shirt.

ONLY

OCCASION CLUBS FROM ONE
TOWN HAVE HELD THE
FA CUP AND RUGBY LEAGUE
CHALLENGE CUP SIMULTANEOUSLY

**WIGAN ATHLETIC 1 MANCHESTER CITY 0 AT WEMBLEY
STADIUM, MIDDLESEX HA9 0WS ENGLAND. 5.15PM
SATURDAY 11 MAY 2013; WIGAN WARRIORS 16 HULL
FC 0 AT WEMBLEY STADIUM, MIDDLESEX HA9 0WS
ENGLAND. 3PM SATURDAY 24 AUGUST 2013.**

On the second Saturday in May 2013, Wigan Athletic upset the odds by beating Manchester City 1-0 to win the FA Cup at Wembley. It was the Latics' first appearance in an FA Cup Final and the Blues' tenth. Ben Watson scored in the 91st minute, the goal coming a few minutes after City's Pablo Zabaleta had been shown a red card, becoming the third player to be sent off in an FA Cup Final. Manchester City sacked Roberto Mancini two days later amid rumours of the manager's fate pre-match while Wigan failed to avoid relegation from the Premier League, becoming **the first team to win the FA Cup and succumb to relegation in the same season**. Wigan Athletic share their ground, DW Stadium, with rugby league side Wigan Warriors. On 24 August 2013, the Warriors beat Hull 16-0, also at Wembley.

DID YOU KNOW?

Wigan, founded on 21 November 1872 in a hotel, is the most successful British rugby league side of all time. The club almost went out of business four years later unable to find top players and had to amalgamate with Upholland. They did go bust in 1879 and a new club was founded in a pub this time.

ONLY

PLAYER TO BE SENT OFF IN THE VARSITY MATCH

Sam Egerton: Oxford 33 Cambridge 15 at Twickenham Stadium, Whitton Road, Twickenham, Middlesex TW2 7BA England. Thursday 12 December 2013

Sam Egerton, a law student at Keble College, Oxford, played his first Varsity match in 2012 and was named man of the match as the Dark Blues ran out winners for the third consecutive year. The following year, he was selected but ended the match in ignominy, as he became the only player to receive a red card in the 141-year history of the annual challenge. Egerton scored a try early in the second half before he was dismissed in the forty-ninth minute for gouging the eyes of Cambridge's second rower Nick Viljoen. At first it seemed as if number nine Egerton was trying to grab his opponent's scrum cap but the big screen replays left Matt Carley, the referee, with little option but to send him off. Despite being a man short, Oxford managed to win 33-15 – their fourth win on the trot. On 17 December, Egerton pleaded guilty to a charge of making contact with the eye(s) or eye area of an opponent contrary to Law 10.4(m). He was banned for fifteen weeks, from 12 December to 26 March 2014.

FIRST

RUGBY SEVENS MATCH AT NORTH POLE

TEAM TIM 17 TEAM OLLIE 14 AT LITTLE FURTHER NORTH THAN THE EXACT 1996 POSITION OF THE MAGNETIC NORTH POLE. APRIL 2015.

A group of intrepid and hardy men became the first to play the most northerly game of rugby sevens to raise £300,000 for Wooden Spoon, rugby's children's charity. Team Tim, captained by ex-international full back Tim Stimpson, narrowly defeated former England 7s player Ollie Phillips's side Team Ollie under the watchful eye of official Rugby Football Union referee Lee Mears, the former England hooker.

Bibliography

Arthur, Max *Symbol of Courage A History Of The Victoria Cross* (London: Sidgwick & Jackson, 2004)

Bath, Richard *The Scotland Rugby Miscellany* (London: VSP, 2007)

Baldwin, Mark *Beaumont's Up And Under* (London: Arcane, 2004)

Bogle, Kenneth and Ron Smith with Allen McCredie *The Green Machine 125 Years Of Hawick Rugby* (Hawick: Hawick Rugby Football Club, 1998)

Bragg, Melvyn *Rich The Life Of Richard Burton* (London: Coronet, 1989)

Cole, Rob and Stuart Farmer *The Wales Rugby Miscellany* (London: VSP, 2007)

Cronin, Ciaran *The Ireland Rugby Miscellany* (London: VSP, 2007)

Dickens, Charles *Dickens's Dictionary Of London 1888* (Moretonhampstead, Devon: 2007)

Farmer, Stuart *The Official England Rugby Miscellany* (London: VSP, 2006)

Fotheringham, Will *Fotheringham's Sporting Trivia* (London: Sanctuary Publishing, 2003)

Gate, Robert *The Guinness Rugby League Fact Book* (Enfield, Middlesex: Guinness Publishing, 1991)

Glinert, Ed *The London Football Companion* (London: Bloomsbury, 2009)

Goodwin, Terry *The Guinness Book Of Rugby Facts & Feats* (2nd edition) (Enfield, Middlesex: Guinness Superlatives, 1983)

Griffiths, John *Rugby's Strangest Matches* (London: Robson Books, 2000)

Hawkes, Chris *World Rugby Records 2015* (London: Sevenoaks, 2014)

Kane, Joseph Nathan, Steven Anzovin & Janet Podell *Famous First Facts* (Sixth edition) (New York: H.W. Wilson, 2006)

Lawrenson, David *The Rugby League Miscellany* (London: VSP, 2007)

Magnusson, Sally *The Flying Scotsman A Biography* (New York: Quartet Books, 1981)

Matthew, H.G.C. and Brian Harrison (Eds) *Oxford Dictionary Of National Biography* (Oxford: Oxford University Press, 2004)

Moorhouse, Geoffrey *A People's Game The Official History Of Rugby League 1895-1995* (London: Hodder & Stoughton, 1995)

Pakenham, Thomas *The Boer War* (London: Weidenfeld & Nicolson, 1979)

Rhys, Chris *Rugby Shorts* (Enfield, Middlesex: Guinness Publishing, 1990)

Robertson, Patrick *The Guinness Book Of Australian Firsts* (Australia: Collins Australia & Guinness Superlatives, 1987)

Ryan, Mark *For The Glory Two Olympics, Two Wars, Two Heroes* (London: JR Books, 2009)

Wallechinsky, David and Jaime Louky *The Complete Book Of The Olympics 2012 Edition* (London: Aurum, 2012)

Weinreb, Ben, Christopher Hibbert, John Keay and Julia Keay *The London Encyclopaedia* (Third Edition) (London: Macmillan, 2008)

White, John *The Six Nations Rugby Miscellany* (2nd Ed) (London: Carlton Books, 2013)

Woolgar, Jason *England The Official RFU History* (London: Virgin Books, 1999)

Websites

austadiums.com

dailymail.co.uk

en.wikipedia.org

englandfootballonline.com

espn.co.uk

espncricinfo.com

fr.wikipedia.org

irishrugby.ie

melrose7s.com

murderpedia.org

peter-upton.co.uk/rugby.htm

rugbyfootballhistory.com

rugbygroundguide.com

thetimes.co.uk/tto/archive

usarugby.org

walesonline.co.uk

yba.llgc.org.uk/

youtube.com